"What Do I Teach for 90 Minutes?"

Creating a Successful Block-Scheduled English Classroom

Carol Porter
National-Louis University, Chicago, Illinois
Deerfield High School, Deerfield, Illinois

National Council of Teachers of English
1111 W. Kenyon Road, Urbana, Illinois 61801-1096

Staff Editor: Tom Tiller

Interior Design: Doug Burnett

Cover Design: Pat Mayer

NCTE Stock Number: 56533-3050

Library of Congress Cataloging-in-Publication Data

Porter, Carol (Carol J.)
    "What do I teach for 90 minutes?" : creating a successful block-scheduled English classroom / Carol Porter.
        p. cm.
Includes bibliographical references (p.   ).
    ISBN 0-8141-5653-3 (pbk.)
    1. English language—Study and teaching (Secondary) 2. Block scheduling (Education) I. Title.
    LB1631 .P63 2002
    428' .0071'2—dc21

                                                                    2002001435

"What Do I Teach for 90 Minutes?"

To my colleagues—John Davis, principal, and the English teachers of Mundelein High School, who are the true authors of this book. Your learning, experimenting, reflecting, and revising changed Mundelein into a place that was good for all learners. Thanks for allowing and encouraging me to record your work.

To my family—Ryan, Michelle, and Tom—who help me create new chapters in my life.

Contents

Introduction

Since block scheduling begins in a different place for every teacher and school, this book is written with an awareness that readers will need to begin in different places and that the information presented does not necessarily need to be read from cover to cover. In some schools, teachers have been involved in decisions relating to the block schedule from the time the idea became part of the conversation. These teachers may be most interested in the chapters on how to revise curriculum and vary instruction for extended class periods (see Chapters 3 and 4). At the opposite end of the spectrum are teachers who hear the announcement about block scheduling in the final days of the school year (or even in the back-to-school letter in August, as we have seen happen in several schools). These teachers may need to temporarily bypass curriculum revision and start with the discussion in Chapter 4 on structuring lesson plans and varying instructional methods. Still other teachers may have heard about a decision to move to block scheduling, or may have been part of the decision, and are ready to begin making the changes necessary for implementation. The first chapter of interest to these teachers might be Chapter 1, "Planning and Preparing: Getting Ready for the Block."

The story of one school's process as it moved from a traditional schedule to the block is described throughout the book as a way to blend theory with practice. Critical areas of preparation for block scheduling are identified and discussed in each chapter section that is followed by reflections titled "What We Learned." Since our process was not perfect, we hope that others can learn from our learning by considering our reflections and suggestions on how we would alter or revise our process were we to prepare for block scheduling again.

When the first change, which led to many others, was made, Mundelein High School (MHS), located in a northwest suburb of Chicago, was a school of about 1,500 students and stood in contrast to the wealth and lack of diversity in surrounding suburban school districts. MHS was named a Blue Ribbon School of Excellence by the U.S. Department of Education for the 1992–93 year. Highlighted in the Blue Ribbon report as an innovation that made our school deserving of this award were the detracking efforts that had eliminated our system of placing students in high-, average-, and low-level English classes. Many factors influenced our decision to detrack. The makeup of our low-tracked classes matched our minority population, which was primarily Hispanic, and we weren't seeing any movement out of the low tracks over the four years students were with us. These divisions of students were just as evident outside classrooms when students congregated in the hallways, ate lunch, and participated in extracurricular activities. Another change and accomplishment that was working in our school was the efforts we had made to reach out to community members by asking them about their concerns, interests, and questions, and by creating monthly parent workshops around these issues.

When the English department made the decision to detrack, we knew we could no longer deliver the same curriculum in the same ways. Our research in the year leading up to detracking focused on how we would need to change our practices. One area of change was to provide more choices in materials and topics of study as a way to accommodate the various "ability levels" in the same class. Other major changes we made included assessing students in more authentic ways through written and verbal responses to literature, highlighting the reading and writing processes in our instruction, rather than attending to the end products of reading and writing by testing reading comprehension and collecting final drafts of final papers; and using portfolio assessment. Interestingly, these are the same curricular and instructional changes that most of the literature recommends to schools and teachers preparing for block scheduling. For the most part, then, we went to the block schedule because extended class periods supported both our needs and our ideas about the instructional approaches we were using in our detracked classrooms.

Initially the request to form parent groups came from students who saw a need for their parents to understand how school had changed since they (the parents) were adolescents. When the groups were first formed for each grade level, topics of concern or curiosity were identified and teacher-leaders arranged monthly meetings with guest speakers. Many topics were dependent on age and grade level. Sophomore parents wanted information on teenage driving, while first-year parents were concerned with dating and homecoming activities. Junior parents wanted to know how to begin the college application process, and senior parents thought they should learn more about life without their adolescents.

All four groups were interested in the curricular and instructional changes that were occurring, so each year the month of May was earmarked for a state of the curriculum address by the superintendent. She shared highlights of the year, along with directions for the future, but most important was her use of this time with parents as an opportunity for instruction: all of the changes being implemented and considered were explained in terms of what educators were learning about learning. The work we were doing with these parent groups also contributed to the Blue Ribbon award, but, more important, it laid the ground work for involving parents in informed decision making related to school reform. They better understood the needs of their children and the constraints that existed within the system, such as traditional scheduling. They began to conclude that if we continued to maintain the same structures in some areas of schooling while trying to make changes in others, learning would be shortchanged.

Another change that facilitated our decision to go to block scheduling started when we were feeling even more inundated with tests than usual. In our frustrated conversations we lamented that testing was driving nearly everything we did. Somehow we were inspired to turn that conclusion into a positive by wondering, What might happen if we changed the assessments we were using in our classrooms? The next school year was earmarked to investigate and experiment with nontraditional forms of evaluating learners. Since we had just detracked our English classes, we worked now to figure out how to grade process and growth in students' work. We also wanted to look at ways in which we could assess students as readers, and, in particular, ways in which we could evaluate literature discussions. Since we were using journaling and other methods of having students respond to their reading, we wanted not only to determine how we could grade these works, but also to figure out how the grading criteria could be used to improve the quality of student responses.

These changes may or may not ring familiar to readers of this book, but they are recounted to make the point that moving to the block schedule will be easier if a research-experimentation perspective and the support necessary for teachers to engage in that type of work is put into place. As an English department, we agreed upon changes we all believed in (detracking and alternative assessments) and we creatively found ways to engage in the learning necessary to begin restructuring. One way we did this was to change the focus of department meetings, and one of the first changes we made in this regard was to read an article for a thirty-minute discussion at the beginning of each meeting. This pushed the "announcement" type of agenda items to the end of the meeting, and eventually these items simply appeared in a memo. Department meetings thus became a time for learning and figuring things out. Eventually our staff development days were organized in much the same way, with teachers finally being given the time and resources that we were giving students when we expected them to learn from their research; we were reading, talking with each other, visiting other class-rooms, and revising our instruction based upon our learning. Many teachers took their research into their classrooms, so while students were doing their research, teachers began to use this time to model the pro-cess by engaging in their own.

What was lacking when we were doing our research on how to move to block scheduling was information on the topic—specifically, literature on how to teach English on the block schedule. We found a few articles and books with general ideas about teaching on the block and then worked together to transfer these ideas to English or to make connections to other methods we were using or had heard about. This book, in turn, will provide some specific ideas to help English teachers know what to do in their classrooms for ninety minutes and will de-scribe a process with which teachers might begin their investigations. While some of the methods described here will be more readily trans ferable than others to any given classroom, we hope that teachers can take pieces of ideas to use as a springboard for revisions as they adapt methods to their own unique teaching situations.

1 Planning and Preparing: Getting Ready for the Block

The literature on methods for preparing to move to a block schedule recommends involvement by representatives from all groups who will be affected by the change (Canady and Rettig 1996; Gee 1997; Hackman 1995; *Illinois State Board of Education Superintendent's Bulletin* 1997). School board members, teachers, students, administrators, and parents should all have a voice in the process. Like other school reform efforts, the decision to change to the block schedule should not be a top-down decision. As we've heard from teachers visiting our school, however, this is all too often the case; a building principal makes the decision, for example, and the school community is forced to make adjustments to accommodate the decision. This chapter addressees two issues—how to involve interested others in the decision-making process from inception to implementation and how to facilitate the ongoing or newly created (in the case of a top-down mandate) adjustments and changes needed in a school to make the block schedule work.

School/Community Decision-Making Process

In the years leading up to our decision to implement the block schedule, our superintendent established community action teams which were charged with determining ways in which the yearly goals of the school could be achieved. In general, the purpose of these action teams was to answer this question: What do we want for the learners in this school? Action teams were established based on key topical areas related to the goals, such as technology, curriculum and instruction, and school climate. Teams were made up of members representing parents, the school board, students, teachers, and administrators. Their work over the first several months of the school year was to learn more about where the school was in relation to the goal, determine where they wanted to be in the next two to five years, and examine possible actions that could be taken to achieve the goals with which they were charged. Teams read literature that addressed issues related to the goals, and guest speakers met with groups to present information directly. Some teams made visits to other schools that had implemented changes or that were known to have exemplary programs related to issues or possible actions the group was considering. The research and learning culminated at the end of the school year with each group presenting its recommendations to the other action teams. Administrators and school staff serving on action teams presented recommendations to the faculty, and we implemented the recommendations over the summer and during the following school years.

Mundelein High School's decision to move to the block schedule was the result of a recommendation by a community action team which found that traditional ways of using time during the school day were inhibiting what could be done for students. We had been changing the delivery of curriculum for three years before the decision to move to a block schedule, due to our previous decision to detrack most of the first-year and sophomore-level academic areas, and the instructional changes we had made as part of detracking helped lead us toward block scheduling. Students were examining, investigating, and discussing topics of study in their work to reach final benchmark projects, exhibitions, and portfolios, and, while it was possible to fit the types of experiences that would lead to these assessments into fifty-minute time periods, longer class periods offered more instructional flexibility and learning continuity.

Of course, other factors were also considered in the action team's decision to recommend block scheduling. Academics were consuming most of our students' schedules, and a tax cap that spanned several years combined with increasing enrollment meant possible increases in class size. The block schedule gave students the opportunity to enroll in more electives and helped maintain current staff and class size, because teachers using the block schedule teach an additional course each academic year.

What We Learned

- Teams need to meet jointly midway through the school year to share some of their discoveries and the directions they are considering. Because of the overlap of issues, a recommendation or plan of action that one group is considering will sometimes have an impact on the decisions of other teams. A joint midway meeting would be a time when teams could see how their plans are leading in similar directions and/or how a recommendation that one group is considering may be a solution to a problem another group is attempting to address.

■ Some decisions like block scheduling were a shock to teachers. When the new superintendent first formed action teams, teachers didn't realize that the teams would truly have a role in decision making—they were not used to committee decisions being carried out—and they didn't necessarily expect that their voices would be heard. Volunteering for committees was not something teachers were compelled to do since their previous experiences with committee work usually spanned several years only to have the issue disappear or to see other concerns become more important before decisions were made. Most recommendations were simply forgotten, and many others were labeled as a nice idea but too costly. If new ways of making decisions are going to be used or if existing structures are going to change, teachers need to know, even if initial announcements are met with skepticism.

■ With the complexity of making the change to block scheduling, not all of the implications of block scheduling were considered before making the decision. This made some departments feel like block scheduling answered the concerns of teachers on the committee, while other teachers and departments felt as if this was a decision that wouldn't have been made had their perspectives been considered. Because of the lack of teacher volunteers on action teams, only certain voices were part of the decision-making process, so teams did not always represent the ideas or concerns of the majority of the teachers. Some departments were represented and others weren't, so suggestions for change sometimes seemed self-serving because of the limited perspectives that were available during discussions. Therefore, we recommend steps such as selecting representatives from each department/division to serve on teams, or creating mechanisms by which to seek input along the way from teachers who are not serving on the committees.

Choosing the "Right" Block Schedule

Many schools consider block scheduling a way to help students prepare for the challenges of the workplace and/or a way to improve school climate. But whatever reason is driving the decision to move to the block schedule—whether it's a principal who is attempting to change the way instruction is delivered, a solution to a state-imposed mandate for increased graduation credits, or teachers finding it difficult to deliver curriculum that addresses the needs of learners in fifty-minute periods—research on the various forms of block scheduling needs to be done. Some schedules, for example, address the concern that English teachers have for the large numbers of students they see each day and the resulting daily paperwork load, while other ways of organizing the school day have been created so that there are no large gaps of time between courses, as can happen, for example, when students have an English course in the fall of one year and then aren't enrolled in another English course until the spring of the following school year. A general description of the most common block schedules follows, but it is likely that no two block schedules being used in schools today are the same. Most schools look at sample schedules as a starting point from which to begin drafting and personalizing a schedule that works for their students and teachers. (See the charts in Appendix A for models of how courses are scheduled in each of the block types discussed below.)

Copernican

Joseph Carroll (1990) introduced the Copernican Plan, named after the sixteenth-century scholar Nicolaus Copernicus, in the early 1970s. Carroll suggested a schedule of two 85- to 90-minute required classes along with one or two electives, all meeting each day for 90 days, after which time students would demonstrate mastery of course objectives. Credit for a course is earned when objectives are met, a plan that challenges the traditional Carnegie-unit-driven schedule of six 50-minute courses per day for 180 days.

Alternate Day

In this approach (known variously as Block 8, A/B, Odd/Even, or Day 1/Day 2), students are enrolled in a total of eight 90-minute classes for the entire school year on an alternative-day block schedule. Each day, four of the eight classes meet. Many schools use the school colors, say, red and gray, to designate which classes meet on which day. For example, four classes meet on red day and the other four meet on gray day. Red and gray days alternate throughout the school year. Although there are day-to-day gaps in instruction with this type of schedule, it offers the advantage of meeting all year long, and it is easier to enroll transfer students. A student transferring in November, for example, has attended approximately forty days of 45- to 50-minute classes at his or her previous school. When transferring to a school on the alternate day block, he or she would have missed twenty days of 90-minute classes at the new school, which is nearly the same amount of instructional time. Transferring to a school on a 4×4 schedule, however, the same student would have missed nearly forty days of 90-minute classes, or one full semester.

Four-by-Four Block (4×4)

On the 4×4 block schedule, students are enrolled in four classes that meet for ninety minutes every day for a "semester" (a time period that usually needs to be relabeled in schools on this schedule). One year's work is thus contained within a traditional-semester time period. Courses that typically earned half a credit or that met for only half a year on the traditional schedule would meet for only nine weeks (one term) on this type of block schedule. Teachers teach a total of six classes during the year but only three classes each day (Schoenstein 1995).

Trimester Plan (3×5 Trimester Plan)

With the trimester schedule, students are enrolled in five classes for approximately sixty days, or twelve weeks. Class periods are usually 70 to 125 minutes long. Some electives that need to meet for the entire year, such as newspaper, yearbook, band, and chorus, meet for 60 minutes each day. A typical teacher load is four classes a day, with about twenty-five students in each class for a total of approximately one hundred students per trimester (Geismar and Pullease 1996).

Examining and Changing the "Nuts and Bolts" of Doing School

As soon as the Mundelein High School (MHS) action team's recommendation to create an alternative schedule incorporating extended class periods was announced, the halls, offices, teachers' lounge, staff dining room, and faculty meetings were filled with a host of "what about" questions: "Well, what about graduation requirements? Couldn't a student graduate in three years?" "What about attendance? One day absent from school would be like missing two days on the block." These questions revealed the genuine concerns of the people who were going to be affected by the block, and these concerns needed to be addressed prior to putting the new schedule in place. Teachers, parents, and students at MHS generated the following list of concerns, recognizing that policies, procedures, and the work we did in relation to these areas would need to change.

- Master schedule
- Student schedules
- Extracurricular activities
- Homework (department policies)

- Open house and parent-teacher conferences
- Flex schedule/compensation time
- Teacher evaluation
- Deans' and counselors' access to students
- First-year orientation program
- Advisory period
- Graduation requirements
- Field trips
- Assemblies
- Add/drops and suspensions
- Grading
- Title I
- Attendance requirements
- Progress reports/semester grades
- Final exams
- Physical education waivers
- Announcements
- Failures
- Student privileges (parking, lunch, entering and exiting building)
- Student support services
- TFC (truant from class) failures
- Makeup time
- Inhouse substitution

Even though forming committees was generally seen as a negative way to address school problems at our school, teachers were beginning to see that committee work could result in action when the principal asked for committee volunteers to address the list of concerns generated by the action-team recommendations. He promised that groups would function for a short period of time—only long enough to arrive at a decision or process to address the concern. Committees were established from a pool of volunteers who indicated their interest in specific issues. As much as possible, meetings were held during common planning and lunch periods and before and after school. Some issues, such as the master schedule and teacher evaluation had a large number of volunteers wanting to serve, while first-year orientation and announcements had fewer numbers of teachers wanting to be involved in the decision-making process. By approaching committee membership in this way, teachers felt like their ideas and concerns were heard, and although decisions might not have turned out exactly as they had expected when they arrived at the first meeting, it was the learning they did in arriving at the decision that made suggested changes acceptable.

Committees approached their decision making from the same research-learning perspective that the action teams had used. Committee members read articles, attended conferences, visited schools, talked to educators with experiences related to the issue(s) they were considering, and shared and talked with each other about all they were learning. Rough draft ideas and the rationale used to arrive at them were presented to the faculty at all-faculty, department, or luncheon meetings and were summarized in follow-up memos. After presenting and gaining feedback, committees met again to reconsider and revise their ideas. Once all committees had gone through this process, final presentations were made and policies established.

What We Learned

- Ideally, membership on committees should include a representative from each department in the school so that all needs and perspectives will be considered in arriving at a decision. When some of the Mundelein committee decisions were presented to the faculty, for example, it didn't appear that they had thought about the decision in relation to the demands on an English teacher or the approaches that are unique to the teaching of English. These perspectives (the realities of our unique teaching situations) could have been considered if, as a department, we had identified one person to serve on each committee.

- Some teachers volunteered for committees for personal reasons—to eliminate certain ways of doing things and/or to make sure certain structures remained the same. For example, some teachers wanted to eliminate field trips, announcements, and passes to the deans and counselor's offices altogether. Serving on a committee with this type of agenda made it important for groups to agree on purpose(s) as related to the issue before arriving at a decision.

- Many teachers and administrators are uncomfortable with the unknown and need to know that there are firm plans in place before making educational changes. They want to be certain that their planning and decisions are going to work—that they won't be in the middle of carrying out the new plan only to discover that a different option would have worked better or that other considerations should have been addressed. The English teachers felt this way several years prior to block scheduling when rewriting the curriculum. We wanted to get it right;

we wanted to make sure we had thought of everything. When our anxiety was at its peak, our superintendent asked, "Is it the best final draft you can create?" The team of teachers responded with a confident yes, to which she replied, "Then that's all you can do—final drafts can always be revised. That will be the work you do next year as you learn more with your students" (Hanson 1992). The same advice held true for block planning—there comes a point in time when you've fine tuned your plans as much as possible. Eventually you have to try them out knowing that with experience and learning you will need to go back and revise.

- Too much planning and preparing for the block can lead to anxiety. Toward the end of the school year in which we planned, we found that many teachers were more concerned than they had been several months before—they just needed to quit planning and start teaching.

Committee Decisions

Tentative answers to the "what about" questions that we had during our 1995–96 planning year can be found in Appendix B. Open forums were held in the spring of the school year prior to changing to the block schedule to give parents and students an overview of how school would be different. New policies and procedures were included in the student handbook, which was distributed to students and parents at registration and open house. We discovered that many of the decisions, once articulated, weren't decisions related specifically to block scheduling; most were effective ways of working with students regardless of the type of schedule. For example, calling a parent if a homework problem exists—one of the block scheduling homework "procedures" outlined by the homework committee as a strategy teachers should use—is a strategy that should be used regardless of the type of schedule.

Although all of the issues listed earlier in this chapter and described in Appendix B will have an impact on the professional life of an English teacher, the decisions that were made about homework, Title I, and field trips are examples of issues that directly influenced the teaching of our English classes. Specific English department procedures on these issues follow the schoolwide decisions.

2 Supporting the Professional Development Process

Most teachers realize that a change to the block schedule means a change in instruction. This realization will affect different teachers in different ways. Some will want to know what to do—what activities will help them to vary the instruction while teaching the same content. Others have been trying methods that were difficult to fit into fifty minutes and thus see the need to change the curriculum to better serve the new objectives and purposes that go hand-in-hand with new methodology. This chapter describes a professional development process that can support all teachers in the changes they will need to make for block scheduling, regardless of what types of instructional methods they are currently using.

Initially, the questions asked by teachers when they first learn about a change in schedule deal with the "nuts and bolts" of how the system will need to change in response to a new way of doing school (Hackman 1995; Cunningham and Nogle 1996). Once these concerns are addressed (see Chapter 1, "Planning and Preparing") and the reality of teaching for extended time periods sets in, concern shifts to the instructional changes that will need to be made. Much of the available literature on block scheduling suggests that teachers should not lecture for the entire class period—instruction needs to vary (Canady and Rettig 1995; Fitzgerald 1996; Cunningham and Nogle 1996); instead, common suggestions include combining of lecture, small group work and/or discussion, and in-class time for reading and writing. (See Chapter 4, "Varying Instruction Approaches.") Creating and supporting a research environment in a school or department as a way for teachers to prepare for the block schedule can help them see, understand, and decide what changes can be made in their classrooms (Wyatt 1996; Shortt and Thayer 1997). The specifics of what needs to be done to prepare teachers for teaching extended class periods will depend on the instructional methods that individual teachers are already using.

During the professional development time that has been set aside for block preparation, teachers who approach reading and writing as a process may want to examine some of the learning experiences they find are getting shortchanged on a traditional schedule. One area of inquiry for such teachers might involve ways to get students to reflect on their learning and their reading and/or writing processes. Another area of investigation might involve incorporating more opportunities for speaking and group presentations. Teachers who have been using lecture as the primary method of instruction might want to find out more about various instructional strategies that can be used when students are reading required novels, short stories, poems, and essays.

Sources of Information

Site Visits

When we were preparing for the block schedule at Mundelein High School (MHS), the principal and curriculum coordinator compiled a list of schools on the block schedule that were willing to work with visitors. Arrangements were made for teams of teachers from each content area to visit schools on specified days. After each visit, MHS teachers who had spent a day observing at a school on the block led discussions during common lunch periods and at department meetings. Being able to see a block schedule in action was probably the most helpful way of preparing teachers for teaching English on the block. They were able to see how teachers structured their time with students, and many of their fears about student inattentiveness in "excruciatingly" long class periods were alleviated. Teachers whose classrooms they visited were able to share firsthand the positive aspects of block scheduling, and they also made suggestions about avoiding various pitfalls.

Guest Teachers

Bringing in teachers from other schools who are teaching English classes on the block is another excellent way for teachers to get their questions answered. If these visiting teachers can stay for several days, they might also teach selected classes using some of the strategies that they have found to work. In our case, teachers who visited other schools that already used block scheduling identified teachers they had observed to spend an inservice day with us. These teachers talked about curriculum revisions and shared lesson plans, but mostly they answered questions raised by teachers in the department.

Books and Articles

Resources related to specific instructional changes that need to be made when teaching for extended class periods can be helpful in preparing for the block schedule. However, these resources are limited in number and often aren't specific to the English classroom. We found that turning to literature on topics related to some of the suggestions for instructional change—such as small-group work, literature discussions, student inquiry and research, and multiple intelligence projects—was helpful as long as we were working together to understand and figure out ways to apply the suggestions to our classroom situations.

Experimenting with Instruction

As teachers observe, hear about, and read about instructional methods suggested for extended class periods, they should begin to try them out within the "safety" of familiar surroundings while all other factors—classroom, students, time schedule, and materials—remain the same. They will need to keep in mind that many of the suggested strategies are more viable when used in extended time periods and that making dramatic shifts in the way teachers and students operate may affect the success of new instructional methods. Support from the department chair—who should also be involved in trying out new instructional techniques and in sharing frustrations, adjustments, and achievements—will also help teachers see that trying new methods is a messy but rewarding endeavor. And collaborating with other teachers who are also trying new methods will give teachers a way to revise approaches so that the methods work in their particular settings while also providing them with a colleague who is experiencing similar challenges and successes.

One Teacher's Experimentation

Brad, one MHS English teacher who was already approaching the study of literature from a reading process perspective, wanted to learn more about literature discussions and student reflection to prepare for the block schedule. Since he felt that the new schedule would offer more opportunities for students to talk in small groups about the books they were reading, he decided he needed to improve the quality of their interactions and increase his knowledge of how to support this type of work. But he didn't want literature discussions to be a structure that was imposed on his students; rather, he wanted students to reflect on their discussions and then use these reflections to decide what types of interactions supported and enhanced their understanding of the text, and which interactions interfered.

During the semester before moving to the block, and while still teaching fifty-minute classes, Brad secured six tape recorders, and students made tapes of their discussions. During the class period following these discussions, students created transcripts in their groups by listening to their own tape and having each person write what he or she had said. Each comment or question was numbered to show the order in which the various remarks were made. Next, the students identified the places where the discussion seemed to "fall apart" and those places where their talk led to some "great ideas," and these portions of the transcript were compared to see how they were different. Students' insights and conclusions were then discussed with the teacher. After these self-evaluations and process discussions, Brad worked with the students to set group and individual goals for their future discussions.

During this time, Brad was also reading articles on literature discussions and observing the ways in which other teachers, who were also experimenting with small group discussions, were approaching this instructional strategy. He used ideas from his research when meeting with literature discussion groups to help them set group and individual goals. By the end of the semester, Brad felt that he was more prepared to incorporate discussion into his instructional plans for the block schedule—an activity that he sometimes avoided on a regular schedule because of time constraints and lack of experience and success with them.

Another Teacher's Experimentation

Teachers whose primary method of instruction has been lecture may want to experiment with approaches such as student inquiry and research, writing process, and infusing speech into the curriculum. Another teacher in our department, Susan, examined ways in which students could conduct their own research on literature they were studying. Along with providing class time for mini-research-projects, she began experimenting with having students give presentations rather than write papers on the information they had gathered.

One approach that started out small was to have students list questions about the literature they were reading on a special sheet she had devised for this purpose. As students neared the end of their reading and were preparing to move into the writing portion of the unit, Susan had students turn in their question sheet, and she then compiled a class list of questions from which each student would choose one. Once all students had a different question, she took them to the library for a day of research. The following day, students shared the answers to their questions in brief, impromptu speeches.

These presentations became a new class activity and eventually formed the basis of a speaking assessment once Susan started teaching on the block. Later, as she began to feel more comfortable with these changes, she altered the ways in which students chose topics for research papers by having them generate their own questions in relation to the literature, authors, themes, and time periods being studied, rather than having them choose from her predetermined list of topics. Like Brad, Susan was reading books and articles, and talking and discussing with other teachers, as she tried new ideas and worked to refine the instructional approaches she was using with students.

Planning for Instruction

As teachers see ways that they can change instructional methods, they can begin to plan for two days of instruction on a traditional schedule as if it were one. For example, one of my literature lessons on Monday involved students in reading, journal writing, and whole group sharing of ideas for discussion. This lesson was followed by small group discussions, large group sharing and lecture, and written reflections on learning the next day. In my lesson plan book, I drafted a plan for how I might structure the same lesson for one class period on the block. I tried to use the same procedure with my Wednesday and Thursday plans and continued using this type of experimentation throughout the remainder of the school year preceding the move to a block schedule. One of my writing lesson plans began with revising rough draft pieces, followed by computer lab work. The next day, students shared their drafts in small groups to gain ideas for revision, and the class period ended by having students revise their drafts. Again, I created a block schedule version of the same lesson so I could get a feel for how to structure an extended lesson. (See Appendix C for lesson plan outlines illustrating time management.)

What We Learned

- Teachers volunteering for visits to schools that were already operating on the block were often the teachers who felt excited about block scheduling and were already experimenting with changes in their classrooms. Their reports back to the department tended to address or have answers for teachers with similar approaches and attitudes. Teachers using more traditional methods in their teaching were affirmed in their belief that block scheduling was not a good idea, either because they still didn't know what to do for ninety minutes or because the ideas being shared didn't seem feasible. Sending groups of teachers with a wider range of approaches would have helped more teachers to see where changes in instruction could be made in relation to where they were.

- Site visits by more than one person provide for processing time as teachers travel to and from sites and meet to plan how to present the information they gathered from teachers at the school(s) they visited. In addition to allowing teachers to share varied perspectives on some of the same observations, such discussion allows them to brainstorm ways that an idea they saw or heard about might work in their unique teaching situations.

- Looking at professional development as time for teachers to read, talk, and plan for instructional experimentation changes traditional inservice and staff development models. It also changes the money needed for such programs. In the year in which we prepared to move to the block, teachers applied to be released from their supervisory period. This time was then used to do the research and work that needed to be done to try out new methods. Paraprofessionals were hired to do supervisory tasks while we were still on the traditional schedule at a cost less than what was typically spent for outside speakers in previous staff development budgets.

- We spent a lot of time searching for books and articles about how to teach English for extended time periods, and when we couldn't find them, we spent an equal amount of time whining about the information we needed and the lack of resources available. Finally, after much valuable time was lost, we went to resources describing some of the general methods suggested for teaching on the block: reading as a process; writing as a process; integrating reading, writing, speaking, and listening; and inquiry-based learning strategies. For example, Nancie Atwell's *In the Middle* (1987) was a great source for teachers who were unfamiliar with teaching writing as a process, and *Reading Strategies and Practices: A Compendium* (Tierney, Readence, and Dishner 1995) contained, as the title suggests, page after page of reading strategies that support a process approach to reading. Several teachers used Daniels's *Literature Circles: Voice and Choice in the Child-Centered Classroom* (1994) to learn more about structures for small group discussion. Ken Macrorie's *The I-Search Paper* (1988) and Tom Romano's *Clearing the Way* (1987) were books that addressed questions teachers had about integration, inquiry-based learning, and choices as they related to writing. Once we became familiar with and actually practiced some of the methods we were learning about in these sources—for example, structures for small-group discussion; group research and presentations; and strategies to support reading comprehension (which also promoted writing and discussion)—we were better prepared for the block schedule. As we think back on our learning, moving to the block schedule gave us the opportunity to learn about, experiment with, and begin practicing all of the methods we had been reading and hearing about but had never found the time to try on a traditional schedule.

- Having teachers identify issues that they want to study will give them a starting point for change relative to where they are. Approaching staff development as research, with teachers being given an overview of some of the instructional changes recommended for block scheduling, will give each person an entry point from which to ask questions related to their beliefs and strengths and the areas they've identified as goals for change.

- It was helpful to team up teachers with similar areas of experimentation. There was more of a sense of "being in this together" and less fear of doing it "wrong."

- Locating resources and arranging visits to other classrooms while teaching a full load will shortchange the teacher learning time that is needed to prepare for the block. Department chairs and curriculum coordinators can best support teachers by locating important articles and strategy descriptions, and by finding ways for teachers both to observe instructional approaches and get feedback on their own.

- Preparing for the block schedule through individual research and experimentation creates teacher experts in areas of investigation. Time for sharing and celebrating individual learning with other English teachers in the department (and ideally with teachers throughout the school) will help teachers to see their progress while providing new information for colleagues to consider for their own classrooms.

3 Examining and Revising the Curriculum

Realistically in terms of the time available to prepare for the block, curriculum revision may need to wait. However, our experience would lead us to believe that teachers will eventually need to spend time revising the curriculum as they continue to learn and try new instructional approaches while teaching on the block. In most schools the existing English curriculum was written with the knowledge that the primary method of instruction would be lecture, with students being assessed through the papers they write and the exams they take. Given the limited time that teachers have with students, and the amount of material they are responsible for seeing that students learn, lecture and whole class discussion are methods that best fit into the fifty-minute (or less) class period (Canady and Rettig 1995). And the assessments that best match this type of instruction are those in which students show that they have learned the material—true/false, multiple choice, and essay exams are the formats that can best be used within the same limited time structures, and they most closely match the instruction provided and content that has been taught.

Thus curriculum, instruction, time, and assessment all influence each other in complex ways. When new ideas for instruction are introduced to teachers who have only fifty minutes with students, a common question is, "How would I have the time to do this?" Conversely, when extended class periods become a reality, teachers typically ask, "What am I going to do with students for ninety minutes?"

Changes in instruction—what is taught and how it is taught—will make changes in assessment a necessity. My own realization of this came one semester at final exam time when I needed to write an exam for my students. It was easy to write questions for the core (required) novels that all students had to read. However, in my effort to incorporate more choice into my lessons, students had also been responsible for reading free-choice novels that either related to the themes and topics of a core novel we had read or were written by the author of a core novel. For the free-choice novels, I was limited to an essay question asking students to compare the themes in the texts of the different authors they had read, or, if they had read several works by the same author, to analyze the author's writing and discuss common elements. I wrestled with how I could I justify only one question for work that had been such an integral part of what we had done all semester, and how differences in content could be assessed on a traditional test. In this same class we had also spent time experimenting with various strategies to support reading comprehension and to facilitate literature discussions. I couldn't figure out how to assess students' understanding of their reading process and the effective group processes they had learned. Without realizing it, my use of new instructional methods had created the need to find new types of assessments.

Less Is More?

Along with the realization that block scheduling necessitates changes in instructional approaches—to incorporate such methods as literature discussions, writing in response to reading, peer responses to writing, research, and individual and group presentations—comes the realization that the amount of literature students read and the number of pieces of writing they produce will need to be reduced (Wyatt 1996). Many teachers question giving up some of the literature students are reading, and they wonder if varying instructional methods is worth the cost in terms of the literature students examine. They begin to feel that block scheduling "waters down" the curriculum.

The usual response to this concern is the "less is more" adage. As an English department, we had trouble accepting this belief at face value and discovered that for us a better way of saying it was this: Students are not learning less; they're learning "different." And it was articulating the "different" that helped us to see that our curriculum was demanding more of students in terms of critical thinking and metacognition and in the written work and presentations we were requiring. For example, using the curriculum in the way it was written on a traditional schedule, American literature students read a Steinbeck novel and three of his short stories, wrote an analysis paper, and took an essay test.

When the same unit and content was revised for the block schedule, various instructional methods suggested for longer class periods were incorporated. Students still read and discussed the novel in small and large groups. However, on the block schedule, small group discussions were a more integral and structured portion of the instruction than they had been on the traditional schedule. After completing the novel, rather than reading all of the required short stories, teachers gave a brief description of each story, students ranked them in order of interest, and groups were formed around each story. Students then studied their story and organized a presentation for the rest of the class. In many classes, students used information from the group presentations to analyze Steinbeck's craft and discuss and/or write a paper about common themes found in Steinbeck's writing.

As the Steinbeck example shows, students read fewer short stories, but the "different" was that they studied one story in depth (with most students going to outside sources in their analysis); collaborated on the information gathered and the meanings they made of the text; synthesized the important aspects of their learning to share with the rest of the class; and planned, prepared, and gave a group presentation. In this example, the "different" learning experiences we added are ones that have always been highly valued in English classrooms. But these experiences and demonstrations require extended time that is less available on the traditional schedule. So students are reading less literature, but they are learning about the literature from others and doing more with what they are reading by developing and practicing valued skills that typically get shortchanged in shorter class periods.

With such a shift in instruction, students are no longer covering as much content in terms of the number of books and short stories they read, but they are learning about the dynamics of group discussion and collaboration, practicing various approaches to group presentations, and gaining experience in various kinds of speaking-to-learn situations (e.g., discussion) and in ways to inform or persuade others (e.g., in formal speeches). A common complaint of teachers who are teaching in fifty-minute or shorter class periods with curriculum written for that type of schedule is that, because they are so busy covering the material, there's no time for students to be thoughtful about what they're learning and how they're learning it. The block schedule offers teachers and students the opportunity to reflect on the content of the course and the processes they are using (and need to use) in order to be successful learners (Canady and Rettig 1995). Time for daily reflection on the strategies that are helping them to learn, and those that are interfering with learning, helps students to understand their learning processes.

So, if we can't deliver the curriculum in the same ways, what do we do? This is the question that typically begins the curriculum revision process, and if your English department is anything like ours was, the next question to be asked would sound something like this: What pieces of literature should our students read? The problem with this question is that it doesn't address the major shift in thinking that goes along with block scheduling. With extended class periods, students have the opportunity to be actively engaged in their learning, which would include individual research, cooperative and collaborative interactions with classmates, and demonstrations of understanding, i.e., performance assessments (Fitzgerald 1996; Canady and Rettig 1995; Wyatt 1996). If students are engaged in learning in these ways, then the question that English teachers should ask is, What do we want our students to be able to do and understand?

Articulating Goals and Outcomes

When I first started my work as department chair at Mundelein High School (MHS), I inherited an office packed with curriculum binders and a storage room filled with textbooks and novels. Typically, my first task would have been to dust and arrange these binders in some order that made sense to me, but I didn't have time for that. I was scheduled to meet with a new teacher to discuss the curriculum and materials she would be responsible for teaching in the classes that had just been assigned to her. We began our work with the ceremonial handing over of the curriculum binder, but what we discovered was a curriculum that was nearly thirty years old. With the exception of the required novels, the curriculum had been written to match the textbooks that teachers were using at that time; as a result, the curriculum had in fact become useless as soon as the textbooks were discarded. We had novels, but when we looked closely at the curriculum goals and objectives, they were specific to the suggested textbook activities; we couldn't find a purpose to guide the reading or teaching of the novels.

The new teacher and I asked several of the teachers who had taught first-year English in the past what the focus was for teaching *Great Expectations* (Dickens 1998), only to discover that each teacher we asked stated different purposes. One teacher focused on methods of characterization and the author's craft, another had students examine the structure of the story as a way to discover how this genre typically unfolds, and still another spent the majority of the time contextualizing the piece in relation to the time period in which it was written and the life and beliefs of the author.

This experience had a great impact both on my own teaching and on my work with teachers. It was at this moment that I realized that materials (and in most cases in English classes, this means the literature) are not as important as purpose. I also became aware of the need for teachers to articulate and come together in their thinking on what purposes should be guiding their teaching. Is it any wonder that we often feel students enter our classrooms unprepared? This sense may in fact derive more from the presence of differing teacher purposes and values than from a problem of teachers simply not preparing students and students simply not learning. Our experience with this curriculum binder also shows that a textbook-driven curriculum is outdated as soon as new materials are purchased, unless it's grounded in a clearly articulated purpose. It's possible that a curriculum can continue to guide teachers in their instructional decisions regardless of the materials being used, if teachers have agreed upon their goals and determined outcomes.

Ask English teachers to articulate one goal that guides their teaching, and most would say that they want students to communicate effectively in written and spoken language. This goal could then be made more specific for each grade level, beginning with the "exiting class," by asking, What do we want seniors to know and be able to do in relation to this goal? Once that question is answered, teachers could ask what juniors would need to be able to do in relation to this goal in order to be ready to accomplish the senior outcomes. This questioning process should continue for all grade levels for each goal that is identified. (See Figure 1 for an example.)

Again, if the English teachers at MHS were typical of most English teachers facing the block schedule and curriculum revision, then the feeling of "We don't have time for these types of discussions; we just need to figure out what we're going to do!" will surface often during this portion of the discussion and planning process. Eventually, though, we were able to see how addressing these questions gave us a framework and knowledge base from which we could determine the changes we needed to make in the curriculum before moving to the block schedule. And once we determined what we wanted students to know and be able to do by the end of their senior year, junior year, and so on, we could see instructional changes that would help students achieve the goals and outcomes. It was then that we were better able to plan for instruction on the block schedule. Once these questions are answered for each goal at each grade level, teachers have a curriculum document with a well-articulated and agreed-upon purpose to guide the decisions they are making about the writing students will produce, the speeches students will give, the instructional strategies that will support them, and the materials that will be used.

Determining Assessments

Thinking about curriculum in terms of what we want students to be able to do (performances or outcomes) at each grade level, along with making changes in the type of work students will do to get to those outcomes

Goal: Students are using reading, writing, speaking, and listening for learning and interacting with others.			
	Objective What do students need to know in order to achieve the goal?	**Writing Demonstrations/ Assessments** What do we want students to be able to do as writers?	**Speaking Demonstrations/ Assessments** What do we want students to be able to do as speakers?
Seniors	Supporting generalizations about various forms of expression using appropriate literary devices	Literary criticism	Panel presentation
Juniors	Considering opposing viewpoints in argument	Expository essay	Persuasive speech
Sophomores	Using concrete examples to support generalizations	Character analysis	Informative speech
First-Years	Using details to describe people, places and events	Personal narrative	Introduction

Figure 1. Sample objectives and assessments for one curriculum goal.

(e.g., small-group discussion, group presentation, and individual research) creates the need for assessments that look different from those English teachers have traditionally used (Wyatt 1996; Wiggins 1989). Since the performances that would demonstrate what students can do and what they understand cannot be fully accommodated in traditional assessments, this is the area of the curriculum that will need the most dramatic change prior to going to the block schedule. And, more than anything else, decisions related to assessment will determine how to vary instructional methods for the block.

When the English teachers at Mundelein established goals for reading (more specifically, goals for determining whether students were using reading for learning), we asked ourselves how we would know if students were accomplishing this goal. Students could demonstrate this skill, we thought, in their writing and in their talk. As a result, our assessments for this goal and for the related objectives included written responses to reading (journals, written conversation, bookmarks, and so on) and literature discussions. (See Chapter 4 and Appendix D for descriptions of these strategies.)

It was at this point in our discussion that we created the framework for curriculum. We structured it the way we did because we were

Goals/Objectives	Demonstrations of Learning/Assessments	Strategies	Materials
			Novels Short stories Poetry Essays Speeches Children's books Drama Art Music Movies Videos CD-ROMs Audiotapes

Figure 2. The framework for curriculum.

determining our goals and objectives first. (See framework in Figure 2.) It also occurred to us that many of the instructional methods (strategies) suggested for teaching on the block schedule that we had been using and reading about could also be used as assessment instruments—for example, our use of the reading strategy of written conversation. With this strategy, our students wrote notes to each other about the literature they were reading as a way to help them better understand the text (writing to learn). What we discovered was that these products were also assessments of their learning. In this way, we began to see that, oftentimes, assessment and the products of our instructional methods could go hand in hand, and in many instances were one and the same. In other words, when instructional methods change, the products (assessments) of student learning will also change. Conversely, when the assessments change, instruction will change in order to support learners in their work to achieve the performances and demonstrations that constitute those assessments.

We were able to fill in the first two columns of the curriculum framework by using the decisions we had made about what we wanted students to be able to do (goals/objectives) and how we would know if they could do it (demonstrations/assessments). For the goal "Students are using reading, writing, speaking, and listening for learning and interacting with others," one of the objectives we identified was, "Students are identifying and analyzing social, historical, and cultural information in various forms of texts." (For other objectives related to this goal, see the "Goals/Objectives" column in the sample curriculum document shown in Figure 3.) For assessments that would show us that students

Sophomore English
"How Does the World Work?"
Core Unit Plan—Terms 1 and 3

Goals/Objectives	Demonstrations of Learning/Assessments	Strategies	Resources
Students are: 1. recognizing point of view; 2. understanding how different points of view are developed; 3. demonstrating how different points of view influence actions; 4. using concrete examples to support generalizations; 5. identifying and analyzing social, historical, and cultural information in various forms of texts; 6. differentiating between perception and "reality"; 7. recognizing that the characteristics of effective communication should be applied to oral presentations (audience analysis, introduction, specific evidence supporting main ideas, conclusion, and awareness of audience during presentation); 8. analyzing their reading, writing, and speaking, and setting appropriate goals.	**Reading** • Literature discussion • Journal • Written conversation • Most Important Word **Writing** • Personal narrative (possible topics: a time when you learned something about how the world works and/or a time when you suffered from social inequity) • Persuasive essay • Editorial **Speaking** • Informative speech **Unit Portfolio** • Essay—Answer to the unit question • Portfolio—Analysis of process and growth in reading, writing, and speaking, with goal setting for future experiences	Authors' circle Freewriting Journal Literature discussion Most Important Word Say Something Speakers' circle Written conversation	**Novel(s)** *Black Boy*—Richard Wright Free-choice novel: Choose from the biography or nonfiction sections of ALA's "Outstanding Books for the College Bound" **Short Stories (Choose 3)** "A Question of Blood"—Ernest Haycox "Crackling Days"—Peter Abrahams "The Parrot's Beak"—Kartar Dhillon "Foul Shots:—Rogelio Gomez "The Interlopers"—Saki "Hitching"—Carlson Vincenti "The Circuit"—Francisco Jimenez "Alien Turf"—Piri Thomas "Nightwalker"—Brett Staples "Meaning of a Word"—Gloria Naylor **Nonfiction** "The Law of Human Nature"—C. S. Lewis "Open Letter to a Young Negro"—Jesse Owens Choose several learning centers in the Advancement Center **Poetry** "A Ritual to Read to Each Other"—William Stafford "A Dream Deferred"—Langston Hughes **Music** "Your Time Will Come"—Johnny Clegg and Savuka (lyrics and tape on file) "Leningrad"—Billy Joel **Video** *The Power of One* "Separate But Equal"—from *60 Minutes*

Figure 3. Fleshed-out curriculum framework for one set of objectives.

had achieved these objectives, we decided on literature discussions, journals, written conversations, and a strategy called Most Important Word, wherein students identify a word that best captures the essence of the text. (See the "Demonstrations of Learning/Assessments" column in Figure 3. See Chapter 4 and Appendix D for descriptions of these strategies.)

Identifying Strategies

When our curriculum teams met, we somehow got off on a tangent—probably the most enlightening learning experience in my teaching career, one that continues to guide my instructional decisions today, and one that I found particularly helpful when planning for instruction on the block. It was a discussion about the difference between a strategy and an activity. Several teachers defined a strategy as something you teach students so they can comprehend their reading. Others saw it as the way teachers approach the teaching of certain skills—somewhat synonymous with a teaching method. One teacher disliked the term because it was used mostly in the context of war and he hated to think of learning as a warlike endeavor. The remaining teachers were irritated with the rest of us for splitting hairs over words, I'm sure, but eventually everyone participated in making a distinction between the two terms.

We decided that a strategy can be used to support and enhance the construction of understandings; it can also be individualized for specific student goals and/or difficulties, and it can be applied to new learning situations. In contrast, an activity is something that teachers might plan into a lesson to create interest in a topic or to change the pace of a lesson, but the student would not be expected to transfer the activity to another learning situation as a method to support learning. The key distinction between these terms in relation to block scheduling is that strategies can be applied to new learning situations, whereas activities are more or less specifically designed for the moment. A teacher who understands and is comfortable working with a repertoire of strategies can make adjustments and create variations to fit the contexts of specific classes, to meet the needs of learners as well as to generate continued interest.

An example of a strategy that Mundelein teachers use with first-year students on the opening days of school is to have each student interview another student in the class, organize the information he or she learned about the person in a cluster or web, and then introduce that person to the rest of the class. Students learn that interviewing is a valuable source of information and that researchers (learners) don't always have to turn to books to learn. The students also use clustering as a way to pull the pieces of information gathered into some type of organizational structure—a strategy that can be used both in gathering information from various sources and in presenting information, whether in writing, speaking, or other formats where ideas need to be organized.

Another way some teachers approach the same opening day is to have students sit in a circle. The first person says his or her name along with an adjective. The next person says his or her name with an adjective and repeats the first person's name and adjective. The same repetition continues around the circle with a new name and adjective being added with each person who shares. Using our definitions, this would be considered an activity—something that is fun and creates interest, but not an instructional method that could be used to support student learning.

As stated in the previous section, most strategies can also be assessed. They can demonstrate a student's understanding and skills. In the interview and introduction example, the cluster could be an assessment related to a student's listening and organizational skills, and the introduction could be an assessment of a student's ability to use listening to learn as well as the student's strengths as a speaker.

With these definitions in place, we then asked ourselves what strategies would help students to make progress toward the assessments we had identified. One strategy that teachers identified as helping first-year students prepare for their personal narrative was freewriting. (See Appendix D for a description.) While reading Annie Dillard's *An American Childhood* (1998), M. E. Kerr's "Where Are You Now, William Shakespeare?" (1983), and selected chapters from Maya Angelou's *I Know Why the Caged Bird Sings* (1983) and Sandra Cisneros's *The House on Mango Street* (1984)—all are personal narratives—teachers had students write about some of their own experiences. These freewrites often related to events that were similar to what students were reading about, or to personal stories they had thought about while reading. Students who had trouble thinking of something to write about were directed to go back to their introduction clusters for stories that emerged during the first-day interviewing strategy.

After completing the required readings, teachers had students go back into the literature to determine some of the common characteristics of the stories they had just read. By analyzing common structures in the personal narrative genre and approaches the authors had used to craft their stories, students developed criteria for writing an effective personal narrative and then used these criteria when going back to one of their freewrites to create a rough draft (Cleland and Wirt 1995).

In sophomore English classes, the strategy of written conversation was used to provide students with the experience of writing to an audience, in this case their reading partners, which gave them a reason to use examples to support their opinions about the texts they were reading. And, when teachers instructed students to focus on characters when they wrote to their partners, the students were practicing much of what they would do later in their character analysis essays. Curriculum revision can be another way in which teachers prepare for block scheduling. For example, in the case of our English department, a list of instructional strategies and alternative forms of assessment that we had read or heard about became topics for individual inquiry. After nearly two months of research, each teacher reported back to the group, and decisions were made about the types of strategies (see Appendix D for a list of strategies) that would best support students in achieving the assessments and/or goals we had settled on. We also considered our major concern with moving to the block when considering and later choosing strategies: Would the strategy help us to vary instruction while teaching extended class periods? Strategies that seemed as if they would support students in achieving the assessments and goals were added to the "Strategies" column of the unit (see Figure 3).

Choosing Materials

Finally, we got to the place in our curriculum revision and writing where we had wanted to be all along. We were ready to examine the content and materials in the existing curriculum documents to determine what would best help students to achieve the goals and performances we had identified for the curriculum we would use on the block. We were now looking at materials in a more purposeful way—as "vehicles" for helping students to achieve the identified assessments (Tafel 1992). Since much of what we were reading and hearing about teaching on the block related to covering less in terms of the literature read, this was an especially helpful decision-making consideration. With this new lens through which to look at materials, we were able to decide that some texts should remain in the new curriculum document and some needed to be discarded to make room for new content and materials.

By expanding our resources to include nonprint texts, we discovered that we could create more opportunities to vary instructional activities on the block schedule. Using speeches (written and recorded), music, children's books, artwork, live performances, video, CD-ROMs, and the Internet as sources of information required different instructional approaches and in some cases different settings which helped break up the ninety minutes. The music and videos identified in the sample unit "How Does the World Work?" (Figure 3) created variety in instruction, for example, when teachers began the class period by playing the tape recording of the song "Your Time Will Come" and having students follow along with the printed lyrics. Students then underlined portions of the lyrics that indicated what the musicians might be saying about how the world works and then wrote interpretations in the margins. Viewing the video "Separate But Equal" provided the students with an alternative text from which to construct an answer to the unit question, and, by stopping the video periodically and using the Say Something strategy (wherein, after a portion of the text is read (or, as in this example, viewed), two or more learners stop to say something to each other), students were discussing the information being presented on the tape.

The materials that were chosen served as a source of information related to the unit questions, but, as described earlier with the first-year personal narrative, most of the written texts students were reading were also chosen because they were models of the types of writing that students were going to be required to produce. These pieces of literature served as models that would help students to analyze and see the different approaches that authors used to write the types of pieces we were expecting them to create. Using the literature as a model for some of the writing that students would do helped them to develop a set of criteria for the components of effective essays of the types they would be writing. For example, since students would be writing personal narratives, the autobiography *Black Boy* and several short-story personal narratives were chosen as required readings (see sample curriculum document in Figure 3). Students used journal writing, written conversation, and freewriting to make personal connections during and after their reading, and these responses to literature became sources of topics for the personal narratives they would write later.

What We Learned

- Grade-level teams need to talk to each other throughout the curriculum writing process. Even though we had created what we came to call a backward map of the outcomes at each grade level, we had first-year teachers revising first-year curriculum, sophomore teachers revising sophomore curriculum and so on.

If teachers are sharing their thinking throughout their planning and writing, then they can make decisions about unit themes (or, in the case of our curriculum, unit questions), instructional strategies, and materials in a connected and coherent way. We discovered that sophomore teachers were considering more of a world literature focus with their question "How does the world work?" whereas junior teachers were going to stay with their American literature focus by using the question "What is democracy?" These decisions had an impact on what first-year teachers considered for their unit question and the types of literature they would consider for their units. First-year teachers had been using a strategy called Authors' Circle (see Appendix D) for helping students during the revision process and they listed this in their curriculum document. To stop using this strategy during the subsequent years, once students had become familiar with the procedure and had developed a common language around it, would be to discard skills and knowledge that students were bringing to the next grade level.

- As English teachers, we tell our students that there is no such thing as a true final draft—we can always go back into a piece of writing and make changes. We find it difficult, however, to allow ourselves the same flexibility with our curriculum writing. As our superintendent reminded us, curriculum will never be "perfect"—at best it is a well-revised "draft" that will undergo further revisions as teachers learn more about block scheduling, alternative assessments, and various approaches to instruction.

- The type of curriculum revisions that will need to be made prior to moving to the block can take place on early dismissal days or on an inservice day here or there, but this would not ideally support the in-depth discussions that are needed. We recommend doing curriculum revision work during the summer prior to block scheduling and doing further revision during the summer following the first year of teaching on the block. Many school districts apply for grants in the beginning stages of preparing for the block so that teachers can be paid for this work outside of the school day/year. Other districts see this type of work as staff development and use their budget to pay teachers for curriculum revision rather than paying for inservice guest speakers.

- Clerical support is essential. Our curriculum planning and writing sessions were initially planned for full days, but we quickly discovered that we were less than productive after four hours. Our brains seemed to match the scribblings, notes, and papers that were scattered all over our worktable. During the first summer in which we revised curriculum, one of us always took our notes home to type and make sense of our ideas. These fresh drafts were the starting point for our next planning session.

Later, once we had the framework (see sample curriculum framework in Figure 2), we were better able to focus our discussions, and we budgeted for clerical help to do the typing of units and support materials. As the curriculum development progressed, there were other needs, such as: typing descriptions of strategies; photocopying selections of stories and poems from our classroom sets; creating files of materials for each unit; assembling curriculum binders for each teacher and for the district office; and ordering and processing new supplies (e.g., some strategies required the use of newsprint, markers, colored pencils, and other supplies that had not been previously used in most English classrooms), professional books, and videos, posters, music, and other nonprint materials (where print sources used to be our only core materials, these new items were now part of the required curriculum). This type of support helped teachers to focus on the other work that ended up on our "To Do" list. For example, one teacher chose to find more music with lyrics to add to our enrichment list. Another teacher read several collections of short stories by multicultural authors and reported back to the group on titles that best matched our units, and still another teacher investigated the multigenre paper (Romano 1987)—something several teachers had heard of and thought might work well with the sophomore curriculum. Without clerical support, we wouldn't have had the time for this much-needed work.

- The ideal curriculum for the block schedule can't be created in the first year, even if the teachers are knowledgeable in the use of diverse methods and alternative assessments. There just isn't enough time to gather and organize all of the materials from various sources, change assessment instruments, and so on.

- Once the curriculum is planned for the block schedule (actually, this recommendation also applies to curriculum that has not undergone revision), it should be roughly mapped out on a calendar. This was particularly true with the 4×4 block schedule, where a full year of English is taught from August through December or January through June. One teacher said that, in the traditional mode, she usually got through the first novel and all of the short stories by Homecoming. On the block schedule, Homecoming approached and she thought she was moving through the curriculum just as she should until she realized that she should have been halfway through the whole "year." The research paper was usually a project that was introduced before spring break, and now she had to begin it before Thanksgiving. This is not to say that each day should be planned with precise activities for the entire course, but we discovered that certain major events in the school year had become guideposts indicating where we needed to be. By placing major demonstrations/assessments on a calendar, we were better able to see where we needed to be at a given time. See Appendix E for a sample of how the sophomore curriculum shown in Figure 3 was mapped, beginning with December and working our way back through to August.

- Divide by two! The type of mapping suggested above helped us to see that our love of literature and our need to hang on to all of our favorite stories, poems, and novels creates a curriculum that needs to be divided by two!

4 Varying Instructional Approaches

Teaching the literature of various time periods, authors, genres, and themes, and providing experiences and assistance with the structures for writing and speaking, encompass most of what an English teacher does. As a result, deciding how to vary instructional methods in the teaching of content and skills related to these materials and assessments will be the primary concern and focus of English teachers when they prepare for block scheduling. A list of methods, along with descriptions of activities, would help teachers prepare for instruction on the block in the short term, but once these activities are used over a period of time teachers and students will become bored. And if the activity doesn't connect to a bigger picture, it will seem like just something to do to break up the class period but not necessarily very purposeful or connected to the what or why of the content or skills being studied. This chapter, then, will provide suggestions and ideas for developing focused instructional strategies to use on the block schedule within a framework that will be generative of new approaches.

Looking at reading, writing, and speaking as processes where students create meaning and demonstrate their skills and the understandings they've constructed creates a context from which to vary instructional approaches. Framing instruction around what learners do when they approach a text (one they're reading or one they're creating) can be a guide for choosing methods. Making the "things" that readers, writers, and speakers do—the strategies they use to make sense of text—more visible, even making them an explicit part of the lesson— allows teachers to vary instruction in a way that will continue to produce ideas for new approaches while supporting students in their learning of the content and skills of the English classroom.

One reading strategy that most English teachers are aware of and use with students is KWL—what I *know*, what I *want* to know, what I *learned* (Ogle 1986). This strategy highlights some of what readers do while reading, and I used it often during the first months of teaching on the block schedule, because the steps involved in using the strategy incorporate a variety of instructional approaches that could be completed in one class period. As a way to introduce some of the short stories in the unit "How Does the World Work?" (see Figure 3 in Chapter

3), I had students brainstorm all they knew (K) about the difficulties that immigrants have in fitting into the mainstream American culture, a topic related to some of the texts they would be reading. (Of course, in our brainstorming, we also had to define what the mainstream culture was.) Students worked in small groups and listed their ideas on newsprint to share with the rest of the class. Another option would be to have them work as an entire class to generate the ideas while you record them on an overhead or on newsprint.

Next, students generated a list of questions about the topic, related to what they wanted (W) to know. Again, I had students generate these questions in small groups, but I could have done it with the entire class working together. I instructed the students to use the questions they'd recorded to guide their reading of one of the short stories. They should be looking for answers to their questions, I told them, realizing that not all questions would be answered and that some new ones would arise. Students recorded the answers they found, along with new questions (and answers), on a chart I had devised for this experience, but they could have just as easily done this work in their journals.

After reading the short story, students shared their answers—what they learned (L)—in small groups, but again, this sharing could have been done with the entire class. At the end of the ninety-minute class period, students wrote a journal entry in which I asked them to reflect on their learning about the immigrant experience and on how the KWL strategy had worked for them.

I have described this strategy for several reasons. First, it shows how a strategy can guide the planning of a ninety-minute lesson and provide the basis for varying instruction. Second, this strategy highlights some of what readers tend to do before looking at the print on a page or after setting the text aside. Reading isn't something that happens just while the eyes are moving across the page. By asking "What can I do to help my students better understand the text before they read?" teachers can begin to find ways to support comprehension and vary instruction (Crafton 1982). Asking what can be done during and after reading will guide teachers in the same way. Third, this strategy shows that reading, writing, and speaking are not separate and distinct processes. Although in this case one entire class period on the block was used to read one short story, the students were also involved in group discussion (speaking), and they were writing. Fourth, the KWL strategy demonstrates the approximate thirty/thirty/thirty division of time that is useful when first beginning to teach on the block schedule. That is, in this example, approximately thirty minutes were used for prereading, thirty minutes for reading, and thirty minutes for after-reading discussion. Breaking instruction into these thirty-minute chunks makes the ninety-minute period easier to manage when first teaching on the block schedule. Finally, though the KWL strategy was explained in terms of reading, it is a strategy that can also be used with writing and speaking. As students prepare for research papers or informative speeches, they can ask: What do I know about my topic? What do I want to know? And, What did I learn? For example, in my sophomore English class, after reading *Night* (Wiesel 1960), *The Children's Story* (Clavell 1981), "Open Letter to a Young Negro" (Owens, 1970), poems and artwork created by children during the Holocaust and collected in *I Never Saw Another Butterfly* (Volavková 1993), and a collection of current news articles and editorials, students chose a social issue that they had read about and/or were interested in investigating. The first day of research (again I used the thirty/thirty/thirty timeframe for planning) began with students listing and writing out what they knew about their topic. Next, they generated a list of questions, and, during the final thirty minutes, students went to the library and/or computer lab to locate one source that might answer some of their questions. During the first thirty minutes of the next class period, students read from their sources, and they spent the second thirty minutes writing what they had learned. The final thirty minutes were set aside for individual choices that included more reading, obtaining another source, revising questions, or continuing their writing. (This and many other strategies mentioned in this chapter are discussed further in Appendix D.)

Reading as a Process

Many English teachers recall the moment in a college or high school English class when they realized from a discussion that there was so much more to literature than the literal meanings they had previously been getting from their reading. Invariably, this moment occurs in a class discussion when several people find special meaning in something that others hadn't noticed or considered important. Usually a debate of sorts ensues, with multiple interpretations being offered, which in turn leads to other connections to the text, comparisons to other texts, and, possibly, what is known about the author. These connections lead to more debates with even more ideas being generated. Some English teachers identify this exchange as the moment when they decided to become an English teacher. It's this passion for the ideas that can emerge from reading that English teachers hope to produce in their classrooms. But this type of talk doesn't just happen—it occurs because readers have reached a certain level of sophistication in how they examine and interpret text, and/or because the teacher has established the conditions necessary for this to happen by supporting readers in the process.

Usually, the first reading of a text is aimed at understanding. After readers develop basic understanding, then they can examine the piece and study it in ways that allow them to notice, among other things, the author's craft, compelling story lines, and specifics about characters. If readers are supported in making sense of the text first, then they can shift their focus to studying it as a piece of literature that holds many varied interpretations (Smith 1995). In other words, readers will be able to see what they couldn't see when they were working to understand.

Many of the reading strategies described below can be used to support readers in their attempts to understand, and to push them toward more sophisticated thinking. In deciding how to support reading and vary instruction on the block at Mundelein High School (MHS), we turned to books and journal articles, suggestions by colleagues at our school or at conference sessions, and methods we observed other teachers using. Just as many of these strategies, however, derived from ideas that emerged once we started paying attention to what *we* did as *we* read, and then devising an instructional approach that pushed our students to do the same thing. By always asking the students how a strategy helped them, and what they liked or disliked about it, and why, we were able to revise some approaches, discard others, and create new ones.

Before Reading

When planning a lesson for teaching a piece of literature on the block schedule, teachers now have time to introduce the piece in any number of ways. This introduction can be a way to help readers begin to develop an understanding of the text before they read it. This is not a new idea in teaching literature, but the difference here lies in the fact that we are using the reading process to guide and help make decisions about *how* the text is introduced. For example, readers usually preview a text in some way prior to reading. This preview may cause the reader to visualize the setting and some of the events that may take place in the story. Other elements—author's name, the copyright, the genre in which the piece is written—also contribute to the meanings readers make before actually reading the text. Using this kind of knowledge of how readers work to comprehend can help us develop instructional strategies that will highlight these processes.

Seeing the story as it evolves is an important comprehension strategy that can't be tapped if the story is outside the experience of the learner. That's not to say that if readers haven't been to the place in the story or experienced the same events in their lives they can't visualize the text. But, if they've never even seen a picture or can't bring one to mind, the reading would be similar to the experience of hearing a description of a friend's trip to a foreign country without being able to look at pictures of what is being described.

One way to fill this gap is to incorporate artwork, photographs, and videos, which can help students visualize period dress, geography, living conditions, and so on. For example, during a social justice unit titled "How Do We Create a More Just and Equitable World?" we put a collection of large, black-and-white commercial prints of the Holocaust—living quarters at the concentration camps, the gas chambers, the room of shoes, and the train cars—on classroom tables prior to the students reading of *Night* (Wiesel 1960). Students examined these visual "texts" and talked about them with other students at their tables. Groups of photos were passed from table to table, with students continuing to talk about what they were seeing and thinking. After examining these pictures, students were better able to predict some of the events that might take place in the story, and they said they could see what was happening as the author described the concentration camp, the living conditions, and the people.

When reading several essays and short stories about American Indians, one teacher's personal video of a drive through the reservations north of the Grand Canyon helped students to better understand the perspectives that were depicted in their reading. Being from the Midwest, they imagined land to be the type that they were used to seeing—flat, rich black soil filled with row after row of corn and beans. The poverty of the land and resources on the reservation was something they couldn't have imagined without pictures.

Brainstorming strategies for situating the text in the historical and societal time period is another way for readers to begin to understand the text before reading. Strategies similar to the K portion of KWL tap into what students already know about a topic. Readers might make a list or a cluster/web—about, for example, the role of women in society during the time period in which Kate Chopin wrote or about the time period in which *A Doll's House* (Ibsen 1992) was set—as a way to begin thinking about how the characters might be depicted and/or what statements the author might be trying to make in the work. Similarly, many students don't get a full understanding of *A Separate Peace* (Knowles 1985) until they recall and/or learn more about private boarding schools and the society that typically comprises the population of students attending them. Students could begin a cluster based upon what they know and then add to that cluster while watching a series of film clips in which boarding schools are depicted.

By conducting mini-research-investigations prior to reading several related pieces or a novel, readers can gain background information that will support their comprehension. For example, in preparation for reading *Kaffir Boy* (Mathabane 1998), a sophomore English class brainstormed all they knew about South Africa—its history, government, and people. They discovered that they couldn't recall very much. Before beginning the book, then, partners chose topics and went to the media center to find answers. This was truly meant to be a mini-research-project, so the students had thirty minutes to do their research, and another thirty minutes were spent with partners providing the class with the answer(s) to each question. Many of the artifacts of this investigation—maps and pictures, in particular—were attached to the classroom bulletin board set up for the novel.

Videos and audiotapes can help students hear the language of the text. Having students watch the video of one of Shakespeare's plays prior to reading another one of his works is a common way to help students who are unfamiliar with the language; at MHS, this was particularly helpful for our second-language students. At the same time, we knew that if we wanted our students to become better readers, they needed to read, and showing videos took away from reading time. On a traditional schedule, watching a video could take nearly four days of class time—time enough for students to read and discuss two to three short stories. On the block schedule, however, only one class period would need to be used, and, even though the video took the same number of minutes, it felt like we were using less time because it was consolidated into one block. In addition, we discovered that we made up for the lost time once we got to the required readings, because students weren't struggling so much with the text. After listening to several of Edgar Allan Poe's works on audiotape, for example, students read other works by the same author with the voice of the dramatic interpretation in their head. And once the students heard Luis Rodriguez read some of his poetry, they were able to read more of his poems with the same volume, rhythm, and articulation in their minds.

Another way to help readers begin to comprehend the chosen text before they begin reading is to explore poetry and children's books on related themes. We discovered one approach for using poetry and children's books to introduce a novel in an overwhelming moment when we were just trying to get by—a revised curriculum and a new schedule had left us with little time to gather together these types of resources. Knowing we wanted to introduce the core novel by reading some poems that were thematically related, but not having time to gather appropriate selections, someone suggested asking the librarian to pull some of the best collections together and put them on carts. These were wheeled into our rooms and students spent thirty minutes going through the books at their tables in search of poems that depicted several of the themes identified in the book they were about to read and marking the ones that seemed to fit. Students then shared their favorite poems with others at their table and from these chose one that their group would read to the class. Not only did the students enjoy this strategy (which we continued to use), but also we were able to compile a list of titles for future reference in much less time than it would have taken us alone.

We used a similar strategy with children's books when beginning a unit geared to the question "What is culture, and how does it influence us?" Not having a collection at school, we asked students to bring in some of their favorite childhood books. Students shared their books at tables, and then we examined them from a critical perspective to identify "lessons" the stories taught us about "right" and "wrong," gender roles, and how cultural beliefs shape who we are. Again, many of these titles were added to our enrichment list, saving us a lot of planning time the next time we taught the unit.

All of the prereading strategies suggested here focus readers by highlighting important aspects of the text they will be reading. What readers bring to the text will influence their interpretations. Give readers a text to read for a test, and they will read differently and take away different information and ideas than they would if instructed to read for discussion or debate. If students are reading to gather information, they should be told to read for that purpose, and they might even be given information-gathering strategies that might be helpful. Students reading a variety of coming-of-age stories could record the similarities and differences in the characters' experiences by using a T-Chart during and after reading, if they know that this is a purpose that should be guiding their reading (see Appendix D for further discussion of this type of approach).

One strategy that both sets a purpose and helps guide readers through the text is Perspective Taking. Roles can be assigned to students before they begin reading, and students then try to read the text as the person whose perspective they are taking would read it. One of the favorite children's books that students brought from home was *The Giving Tree* (Silverstein 1964). This book was read aloud after students chose the perspective of the tree or the boy. The discussion that followed the oral reading ranked as one of the most spirited and engaging conversations students had. Some students were mad because we had "ruined" one of their favorite childhood stories—they could never think of it in quite the same way again. Many of the boys in the class were uncomfortable with the feminist perspective that emerged, and a few students were able to see the parent-child relationship in a different way after discussing the book. Students who had been reluctant to share even one idea during discussion now engaged repeatedly. They said this was due in part to the fact that they had identified with their character and that they felt comfortable sharing because they were the experts on their perspective. Another use of Perspective Taking is to create character scenarios, where brief situational and attitudinal descriptions are distributed to students prior to reading. A third approach is to have students choose a type of person—say, an artist, a coach, or a news reporter—from a list that the class develops, and a fourth option is to have students assume roles of characters and/or authors from other literature they've read.

During Reading

One of the best things about block scheduling is that time is now available to engage in one of the activities English teachers most value—reading. Since it's difficult on the traditional schedule to justify spending a whole class period reading, this activity becomes one of the most common homework assignments. It's unfortunate that what we value is what we have students do outside of school. With the extended class periods that block scheduling offers, a portion of the period can be used for reading, which can be followed by discussion. This not only shows students that we value reading, but it also assures that all students have read, which facilitates better discussions for comprehension, because the text is fresh in the minds of readers and the questions are fresh—readers are still curious about the answers.

Most of what readers do while reading takes place in the head, but there are some instructional strategies that can support comprehension while students are reading and provide variety in the day-to-day methods that are used on the block schedule. Any format for recording ideas after reading can (and probably should) be used while readers are reading. Again, the ideas for strategies to use while students are reading come from teachers being aware of their own processes and then determining ways to replicate these processes in their instruction.

In most schools, students don't get the opportunity to read in authentic ways, because they don't own their texts. One of those authentic approaches is to mark up the text. How can they learn highlighting or underlining skills, or writing in the margins, unless we give them texts with which they can do this? Photocopying short stories or an occasional chapter from a novel and leaving wide margins gives readers a chance to record their thoughts while reading.

Self-stick notes are another way to mark a text while reading. Students can identify portions of the text that they want to reread or where they had questions, found information related to their purpose for reading, discovered an interesting quote, or located items they want to share at discussion time.

Writing or representing ideas in some fashion while reading is another strategy readers use while reading. Journals or learning logs, Bookmarks, and Written Conversation (see descriptions in Appendix D and in the next section of this chapter) can all be used as readers think of something that deserves figuring-out time or generate ideas they want to hold on to. Many students prefer to draw an image that comes to mind, a symbol representing an idea that was considered, or a metaphor they've thought of. A strategy called Sketch to Stretch (Harste, Short, and Burke 1988) provided the best version we found of this process. Students can record sketches in their journals or on a sheet of paper kept next to them or tucked into a book while reading.

Stopping while reading and talking about the text is another strategy readers use to help them comprehend while reading. Say Something, a strategy where a portion of the text is read and then two or more readers stop to say something to each other, is another during-reading strategy that can help students comprehend the text (Harste, Short, and Burke 1988). This can be done with a short story or informational piece where sections or pages are read silently (or aloud with a partner) and then students stop at agreed-upon points to talk before proceeding with the next part of the text.

Say Something is particularly effective to use while reading a text aloud to the class. Our students, regardless of grade or ability level, like to have the first chapter of a novel read aloud as a way to make sure they are understanding. This strategy can generate interest from the beginning of a novel, and sometimes it is needed in order to motivate many students to continue reading. We also found that reading the last chapter aloud and stopping at various points to have students talk to each other, or "say something," was an effective and exciting way to end the book. ReQuest, a strategy used in much the same way as Say Something, focuses on reciprocal questioning during reading as a way to support student understanding of difficult texts.

As stated in the previous section, the purpose that has been set prior to reading can guide the way readers approach the text and the ideas they pull from it. For example, when we had students reading a text for characterization, we gave them a Graphic Organizer on which to record the information as it was uncovered in the text. Teachers teaching the elements of plot might provide a Graphic Organizer of some sort that would help students record information as the plot unfolds in the story and thus would serve as a guide during reading.

After Reading

The purpose that has been established before reading should guide what is done after reading. Students can use writing or any other form of representing their ideas after reading in many of the same ways suggested in the "During Reading" section. The difference might be that when using these strategies after reading they would explore ideas in more depth or detail. And again, students will often share their after-reading ideas with other learners.

One strategy we used for having students record their ideas during and after reading chapters in a novel is called Bookmarks (Watson 1978). Cutting 8½-by-11-inch sheets of paper in half lengthwise creates two bookmarks that students can use for the same type of writing that they might record in a journal. The difference is that these are often more easily available if they are placed inside a novel. We found this strategy useful when we were first having students write in response to their reading, because the size of a bookmark was less intimidating than a full sheet of paper. This was also a strategy to get students to write during reading (because a bookmark was right there in their book). As an after-reading strategy, we required one bookmark for each chapter.

Written Conversation (Harste, Short, and Burke 1988) is an after-reading strategy that students particularly enjoy because it capitalizes on an activity they engage in quite naturally—writing notes to their classmates. In this strategy, readers simply write a note to a partner after reading and then exchange notes and write a response. These conversations can take place on paper or on computer and can be exchanged with someone else in the class or someone in another class.

Since a portion of the curriculum at Mundelein identified core pieces that all students would read, we could arrange to read some of the same materials on the same day and exchange notes between, say, third-period junior English classes—it simply required that notes were ready to pass across or down the hall at an agreed-upon time. Another variation of this strategy is to take students to the computer lab to write a note and then do "musical chairs" as a way to move to another computer and respond to the original author's ideas. Of course, partners can also be assigned, and, for most students, this provides a different learning experience, since writing to someone you know is different from writing to an unknown partner. Written conversation beyond the classroom can also be done through e-mail exchanges. Yet another option begins with the teacher, who writes the first part of a letter on a sheet of paper that is then photocopied for each student in the class (it can also be written on an overhead transparency). This approach can help assure that students notice or consider certain aspects of the text that the teacher thinks are important.

In order to study literature beyond "just understanding it," readers sometimes need to go back into the text to reread. One strategy that students enjoy is what we termed Quote-Response. With this after-reading strategy, readers go back into the text and pick a quote from the reading. This quote might be a favorite line or the sentence that best answers one of the class questions. It might also be the passage that best depicts the theme or best describes a character. Again, whatever purpose has been set could guide the choices students make. Once students have chosen their sentence, they should record it in some way and write about it. This strategy is a great way to have students prepare for and enter into discussion, which often begins by students sharing their quote and talking about it.

A variation of this strategy is Most Important Word (Padak 1992), wherein the reader describes the essence of the chapter, story, or essay in one word. We usually had students write their word on an index card and then flip the card over to list the reasons for their choice. The students then entered discussion by telling the group their word choice and sharing their reasons. At the end of discussion students could choose a new word or stay with their initial word, or the group could work toward consensus on a word. Their final choices and their reasoning could be recorded on a piece of paper, either in their journal or on a new card.

Save the Last Word for Me (Burke in Harste, Short, and Burke 1988) is an approach for sharing quotes identified when using the Quote-Response and Most Important Word strategies. Students bring their chosen word or quote to the discussion, and other group members respond. After everyone has shared their reaction or the meaning elicited from the quote or word, the person bringing the chosen text to the discussion gets to have the last word.

Most Important Word is especially useful in helping students make sense of and discuss poetry. Copies of poems can be photocopied, and a Most Important Word can be chosen for each stanza and written in the margins. This can be done individually, with a partner, or in groups. After determining the meaning of each stanza, a word can be chosen for the poem as a whole.

Most of the after-reading strategies described here can be taken into discussion as springboards for the ideas that are shared. For example, with any of the writing-to-learn strategies, students could mark one or several of their ideas to share with their group by highlighting, underlining, or starring these in their writing. After discussing these ideas, students can record the ideas that were generated by the group in response to the ideas they brought to the table.

If a theme or unit question has been identified as a focus for the materials students are reading, a portion of some discussions could focus on how the text relates to the theme or helps to answer the unit question. Again, the purpose that has been established before reading should guide what is done after reading.

Another format for discussion is to have students draw symbols or sketches to represent the theme, or a character, and then share their results with the group. Using the Save the Last Word for Me process, each group member explains what he or she sees in the symbol or sketch and offers an interpretation of what is being depicted. After everyone has talked about the drawing, the person whose sketch is being discussed tells the group what he or she intended and shares any new ideas sparked by the discussion.

Posting questions on an inquiry board whenever they arise is another strategy that was easier to use once we were on the block schedule. When questions arose that couldn't be answered during discussion or while reading, we wrote them on pieces of construction paper and attached them to a bulletin board created especially for this purpose. Eventually, these questions were used for a mini-research-experience where students chose a card from the board, spent a portion of the class period finding an answer, and then explained the answer in an impromptu speech.

Below are two sample lesson plans that incorporate some of the suggested before-, during- and after-reading strategies.

Day 1

30 min.	Read children's story aloud to the class using Say Something strategy.
45 min.	Read Chapter 1 of novel aloud to students.
15 min.	Written Conversation—Have students write notes to assigned partners, exchange, and write responses.

Day 2

5 min.	Identify areas in Written Conversation to discuss in small groups.
20 min.	Discuss Chapter 1.
35 min.	Read Chapter 2 (identify purpose for students so they can focus their reading).
10 min.	Quote-Response—Have students go back into the text to find a quote that best matches the purpose that was set.
20 min.	Share quotes in discussion.

What We Learned

- Using reading strategies as a way to vary instruction on the block can promote the teaching of reading and improve students' reading skills. By the time our students were juniors and seniors, they read more and were reading more difficult materials than they had been prior to the changes we made in our instruction. Any loss of content (literature) caused by focusing on before-, during-, and after-reading strategies was more than made up for over time.

- Taking time during department meetings to talk about the strategies we were using helped us to see that there are many ways in which teachers can approach a strategy. Again, this was one of the most beneficial ways for us to continue to prepare and continue to learn new and varied approaches for teaching on the block. The strategies we discovered and shared were written up and compiled in a strategy book (a project one teacher took on for a graduate class) as we learned more about reading, discovered new variations, and gathered student samples.

Writing and Speaking as a Process

Writing and formal speaking are discussed together, because the end product of both processes is a text in either written or spoken form. Preparation for formal speaking assignments usually requires that students create a written draft that goes through much the same process that other types of written texts go through. With the exception of how the final draft is delivered, many of the genres or formats are similar for writing and speaking.

On a traditional schedule, teachers usually discuss in class the topics for writing and speaking as well as the specific formats to be used, and students typically produce the assignment as homework—again, as with reading, time constraints cause us to relegate what we really value to the realm of homework. On the block schedule, however, time is available for writing and preparing speeches during class. As suggested with reading instruction, teachers can examine what they do before, during, and after drafting a text as a way to create instructional strategies that both support writers and vary instruction. Much has been written about the various prewriting, drafting, revision, and editing "stages" of writing, and most teachers have incorporated these or related strategies into their writing instruction.

The teachers at Mundelein had been highlighting the writing process for many years before going to the block schedule, but we had never had the luxury of putting all of the parts of the process together for students during one class period. Typically, we had provided instruction on format and put students through prewriting activities during one class period, then required that they write a draft as homework. The next day, we would try to do some form of peer feedback so that students could get ideas for revisions that they would work on as homework. (I use the word "try" because theoretically we believed in the value of peer feedback, but instructionally it was never one of our strong points.) So, when we started planning for the block schedule, we decided that we would look at everything writers do when they write as a potential in-class activity that we could highlight in our instruction, realizing that our biggest challenge was figuring out how to improve our methods for helping students learn to revise their work.

Because we could go directly from a prewriting activity to writing a rough draft in the same class period on the block schedule, we discovered that students didn't lose momentum between prewriting activities and their rough draft. They were also better able to work their way through stumbling blocks in their writing knowing they would be able to get ideas for revision from their peers during Authors' Circle (Harste, Short, and Burke 1988), the instructional strategy that we eventually began to use for peer feedback, as described later in this chapter. The writing process became more cyclical with less distinction between the stages once we had extended periods of class time, because we had the time to personalize the process or attend to the specific needs and questions of writers as they arose.

Discoveries from Experimentation with Writing and Speaking as Processes

It wasn't easy for us to give time for writing in class or to spend class time for repeated peer feedback (Authors' Circle) discussions. In the backs of our minds we knew that we didn't really have more class time—the block schedule only created that illusion when planning for a class period. We thought that if we were now incorporating all aspects of the writing process within class time, it would mean we had to give up other content. And, we were already feeling like we had given up too much content with the reading strategies we had incorporated into the literature portion of our curriculum. But we discovered that much of what we had been doing with reading—the processes we had highlighted and the work students had done—prepared them for the writing and speaking assignments they would be required to take to final draft.

In revising our curriculum, we had been aware of choosing materials that could serve as models for the written work and for the speeches students would give. But without being aware of it, we had integrated our own "content" areas of reading, writing, and speaking. And, it was this integration that gave us the gift of time that we were able to use for writing in class and getting feedback for revisions before the final draft or performance.

As with reading, we found that outside sources helped us determine strategies to support students when they were writing or preparing for a speech, but we also learned to rely on our own experiences as writers and speakers to guide the instructional decisions we made for students. For example, we knew from experience that having an understanding of the structures for a required piece of writing or a formal presentation helped guide the drafting process; the guidelines that our university instructors gave us were helpful, but they weren't enough. We often asked for or went in search of papers that had been written for the same purpose and/or audience. An in-the-head analysis of these pieces usually got us started on our writing and pushed us in certain directions throughout the process. Rather than having a few students figure out how to do this on their own (in the same way we had stumbled onto this strategy on our own, outside of any classroom structures), we decided to make it part of our instruction.

We had all had the bloody paper experience (well, most of us had), and knew this wasn't an approach that fostered an understanding of our strengths or processes, nor had it helped us to set goals for what we should do the next time we had a writing assignment. Reflecting on our processes also led us to the conclusion that writing improvement occurred most often when we were aware of our processes and our strengths; we could tap into and use this knowledge when writing. Our reflections made us aware that our weaknesses were areas we usually dealt with during the revision and editing stages—most often alongside another writer. But true understanding of what needed to be done with our writing or speaking was a personal reflection based on informative feedback from others.

The remaining sections of this chapter were written with the assumption that teachers reading this book understand and use the writing process in their work with students. For any who don't, many sources are available that describe how to teach writing as a process and that provide instructional strategies to use with students. In lieu of repeating these approaches in this text, a list of writing process resources can be found at the end of the chapter. Most of these recommended sources will not discuss writing instruction in terms of the block, but longer time periods with students should make most of the suggested approaches seem doable. The remaining sections of this chapter discuss details and examples of the discoveries we made in our experimentation and research that both supported writers and provided us with many more and different instructional methods than we had used in the past. We found that a number of instructional changes that would have been difficult to implement on a traditional schedule were much easier to work with in the extended periods of time we had with students on the block: creating assessment instruments with students; integrating reading, writing, and speaking; experimenting with new approaches for revision of writing and speaking; and conducting goal-setting conferences.

Assessment Up Front

When it was time for first-year students to write their personal narratives or for juniors to prepare for their persuasive speeches, we pulled sample papers and videos from some of our former students. These samples represented a wide range in terms of the standards that should be met. Pieces of writing were reproduced and given to students to analyze individually or in groups to determine what the writer did well and what the writer could do to improve. Much of this analysis was informed by discussions we had conducted about many of the personal narratives students had been reading as core literature in their units.

These analyses were shared with the entire class while the teacher recorded student comments on an overhead, on newsprint, or on a computer with LCD projection to an overhead screen. The recorded ideas served as the beginning of a personal narrative rubric that would be used to grade their papers. (See Appendix D for more on the strategy we titled Inductive Analysis of Quality Materials; the discussion includes a step-by-step description and a student worksheet.)

The same general process was used with formal speaking assignments after students watched video clips of the types of speeches they were going to be making. This approach to preparing for a piece of writing or a speech while teaching on the block went beyond having a new method to use during an extended class period. Students began writing their rough drafts with the rubric they had created close at hand, or at least fresh in their minds. The rubric was also helpful to parents and resource teachers who wanted to help their students. Even though these rubrics had the same components that teacher-created ones had always had, students took more ownership in their writing and had more confidence in their speaking when they helped generate the criteria. Eventually, as students began to understand the revision process, they began to use the grading criteria that had been established to guide Authors' Circle and Speakers' Circle comments and revisions.

Integration

Typically we began our units by "reading" the core "texts" (whether novels, short stories, plays, music, visual art, spoken-word audiotapes, or films or videotapes) before moving on to the writing and speaking requirements. When we had students open their folders containing all their work to date, hoping that they might discover ideas for written and spoken assessments, we found that most of the formal writing and speaking assessments were already started, because they connected to the materials that students had been reading and studying. As readers, they had written responses to the literature (Bookmarks, journal entries, Written Conversations, and Quote-Response sheets) and reflections on ideas that had come up in discussion. For example, two suggestions for research were made in the reading section of this chapter that could be used as a rough draft for a piece of writing or a speech. The mini-investigations suggested as a before-reading strategy and the inquiry board that was used for a mini-research-experience could be used as a pre-writing strategy for a formal piece of writing or an informative speech.

Many of the readings in our sophomore and junior curriculum elicited strong opinions from students on social issues and democracy.

Students often expressed these opinions in the various written formats suggested for during and after reading. Encouraging students to go back to these responses to literature and do further research on an issue or find alternate perspectives was another way in which reading, writing, and speaking were integrated as students took the ideas from reading to begin a persuasive essay or speech.

A Graphic Organizer for identifying character attributes after reading was also used as a way to begin a rough draft when students began writing their character sketches. Other Graphic Organizers—such as the T-Chart that was suggested for recording similarities and differences between pieces of literature, topics, or characters—were used to prepare a comparison/contrast paper.

Some schools are now working with essential questions at each grade level or in each course. Students could be required to answer one of these questions in an essay. The Quote-Response strategy suggested for use after students read a text and before entering discussion can be used as part of the process of writing a rough draft, if students have been previously instructed to choose quotes related to the unit question, essential questions, or a theme. In fact, this strategy is particularly useful because students have already pulled quotes from the text after their reading which can then become the supporting evidence in their essay. With the Quote-Response strategy, they had also written an explanation of how the quote related to the unit question, which further helped them with their expository essay. Our curriculum and assessments were even further integrated when we finally figured out that informative and persuasive speeches don't need to be separate topics from the expository and persuasive essays and the research paper.

The biggest surprise to us was the degree to which the discussions we had incorporated into our reading instruction supported writing and formal speaking. When we thought of our own experiences, we realized it shouldn't have been such a surprise. At the time, several of us were commuting to classes at Chicago-area universities. On one of the few occasions when we had to travel in separate cars, we realized that our car discussions after class were helping us put our ideas in concrete form before we put words on paper. We saw this happening in our sophomore English classes, too, when we asked students to bring in several of their favorite photographs to share with classmates as a community-building strategy that connected to a culture unit. Each day for the first week of class, students described one of their pictures to a partner, and the partner asked questions, which they took the time to answer. This telling and question answering guided their writing of rough drafts, because they had already expressed the main points and had gotten feedback from an audience on what information was necessary for understanding and what was most interesting.

Clustering was another strategy that served effectively in various parts of the curriculum. We taught clustering to students from their first day in first-year English, where they interviewed a partner and then created a cluster or web by categorizing the main points and adding details that were discovered while talking to the other person. These clusters provided a way to hold onto ideas which students could then use to organize information for an informal or formal introduction or for a piece of writing that would be displayed on a bulletin board with individual pictures of students attached. As students continued to use clustering and other Graphic Organizers while reading, these too served as sources for their written work and speeches.

Revising Rough Drafts

Most English teachers are familiar with some form of peer sharing of writing to assist in the revision of rough drafts. But, as much as most of the teachers at Mundelein believed in peer feedback, we rarely felt that students benefited from the sharing time. Most of the time it seemed as if students were just going through the motions because they had to. It wasn't uncommon for students to respond to the reading of a peer's draft with, "It's fine, you shouldn't change a thing." And, of course, with such "helpful" responses it was no wonder that the final draft wasn't different from the rough draft—it was just neater. Discouraged, but still believing in the process, we looked at block scheduling as giving us the opportunity to teach the skills necessary to both provide effective feedback to other writers and use suggestions to improve written drafts. (A version of revising for speaking is described later.)

Once we went to block scheduling, we decided that the first piece of writing to be taken to final draft could go to an Authors' Circle in which the entire class participated. In this way, we hoped to teach all students the skills needed to provide effective responses. Each author in the circle read his or her draft aloud while the other authors wrote questions about aspects of the writing that weren't clear, that needed explanation, or that they were curious about. They also identified one aspect of the writing that they found particularly interesting or well done. A form for writing these types of responses was created to guide students in providing effective and appropriate feedback (see Appendix D).

Once the paper was read and classmates' responses were written, students went around the circle stating what they liked about the piece and asking one of their questions. Questions were answered by the author because of our discovery that verbal rehearsal helped students apply revisions to their rough draft. In this first all-class Authors' Circle, students received as many questions as there were students in the class, unless of course some questions were shared among these people. If this was the case, the author had some important feedback to consider; it must be an important question to use for revision if more than one person had asked about the same thing. Once everyone had responded, forms were passed to the author, who would later use these when revising. In a class of twenty-five to thirty students, this process would obviously take several class periods, especially since a full ninety-minute class period couldn't be devoted to this; other activities needed to be planned for variety.

Even though we as teachers were modeling the types of responses that were helpful for revision, there were some students who just "didn't get it." After the first day of sharing, we made photocopies or transparencies of various responses and analyzed these as a class so students could see the types of questions that helped writers revise. Students also analyzed the twenty-five or more responses they got from their classmates for the same purpose. Although a large chunk of instructional time was devoted to this strategy when we first introduced it, time was saved later in the term when students were able to work independently in small groups as they finished rough drafts.

Speakers' Circle

The same process for revision was used with the formal speeches students wrote and presented, but this was more of a two-part process—one that addressed the content and, later, after students had taken the time to practice the speech, another that addressed their delivery. Many of us recalled the days in high school when we practiced our speeches by ourselves in front of our bathroom or dresser mirror, and we were hearing about some of our students doing the same. Just as many, if not more, of our students were hastily finishing their drafts minutes before stepping up to the podium. By highlighting the process that speakers use to prepare for a formal speech, we were able to create instructional strategies that made the process more visible for all students. The practicing and rehearsing to revise performances that used to go on "behind closed doors" became practices we made available in the classroom.

Another discovery we made when reflecting on our own process was that seldom in our professional lives did we speak alone—group presentations were more typical and visual aids were more common in our presentations than were the formal, individual speeches we had given in high school and college. We asked friends and spouses in the business world if our conclusions were applicable to the world outside of education and found that there was more of a balance between formal individual and group presentations in most professions. We were told that most business presentations were heavily dependent on visuals—more so than what we had experienced. Our old curriculum didn't require any group presentations, so this was a change we made when we revised the curriculum for the block schedule. Of course, once we added group presentations, instruction changed, because students needed time to do the research, plan and organize the parts of the presentation, prepare visuals, and rehearse.

Sometimes students were grouped by topics chosen for the mini-research-projects associated with their reading. Other times, we used a strategy called Jigsaw, in which groups read part of a core requirement and then presented it to the class. For example, in one class the teacher read aloud to the class several of the beginning chapters of *The House on Mango Street* (Cisneros 1984). Groups then chose two chapters each and created scripts from the vignettes to perform for the class. The experience with this book culminated with the teacher reading the final chapters aloud to the class.

Students in our classes particularly liked poetry studies where they chose a poet, time period, or theme to study and then presented dramatic interpretations along with analysis, visuals, and information on their topic. For example, in one English class a group of students chose to read poetry by E. E. Cummings and learn about his life, while another group decided after reading the poetry of Siegfried Sassoon and Wilfred Owen to read more war poetry to determine common as well as conflicting messages that the poets were presenting. Still another group, influenced in part by some of the musicians they listened to, and to some extent by their parents' recollections, chose to look at the popular poets of the 1960s to discover the concerns of writers during this time of social upheaval. In their presentations, they made connections between the lyrics of the music they were familiar with and the poems they were reading.

Reflecting on Learning

Teachers often feel guilty that reflection—an important way of thinking about learning experiences in order to set goals for new skills to learn as well as to determine strategies that support the learning process—is typically shortchanged on the traditional schedule. The end of the class period always seems to arrive before anyone realizes it, and there's little or no time for reflection. When teachers begin to plan for new instructional methods on the block, they usually relax a bit about figuring out what to do for extended class periods when they realize that reflection can be built into the end of each class period and can become as common as taking attendance.

In our first weeks on the block, we encountered a few problems with reflection that were surprising but easy to solve by putting a few strategies into place. Our first surprise was that unless we had a specific approach to use for reflection built into our lessons, we ran out of time. We wondered if we had misplaced our blame when we had previously thought that the lack of active reflection in our classes was a time problem. We also discovered that reflection is a skill that needs to be taught to many students; it isn't something that just happens. Our third discovery was that, aside from instructing students to write about what they were learning, or how they approached the reading, writing and speaking activities, we didn't know how to help our students reflect.

A strategy that we easily connected to reflection was having students talk about their learning. We were in fact doing this ourselves when we read aloud to students and shared our pieces of writing as a way to model or teach our process, but we just hadn't thought of having students do the same thing. Thus we realized that a variation of Say Something, where partners usually read and then stop to talk to a partner, could be used for reflecting on learning at the end of a task rather than at the end of the class period. Some teachers taught this skill by having tables of students share one new idea and/or one discovery about they learned. Teachers can also jump-start students' thinking by asking the class questions such as the following:

- How did this strategy (e.g., Quote-Response) work for you?
- What did you discover about the literature or your writing process that you might not have learned had you not used this strategy?
- What did the strategy cause you to do that you usually don't do as a reader/writer/speaker?
- What did you like about it?
- What might have been difficult?
- Are there any other ways we might work with this strategy?
- Are there any other situations you can think of where you might use this strategy?

Hearing the responses of classmates to these questions, as well as the follow-up comments that teachers provided, helped students to understand reflection and its purpose. These reflection discussions also helped to improve the quality of the written reflections that had previously been our only strategy.

Using exit slips is a common strategy for written reflections. Index cards can be used to record questions on one side and discuss new ideas and/or process on the other. A variation of the exit slip is the strategy of Three Plusses and a Wish (Watson, Burke, and Harste 1989) where students record three positive aspects of class on that day or during that week, along with one wish that they have. Teachers can focus these comments or leave them open-ended depending on the purpose.

Many authors have included reflective questions in their journal articles and books, and these can be typed on a sheet of paper and distributed to students. We particularly liked Stephen Brookfield's (1995) questions and so we distributed a typed version of them which students kept in their notebooks for reference. (See the list of "Checking-In" Questions in Appendix D.)

We had been using portfolios as a strategy for reflection prior to block scheduling, but we had struggled with getting students to reflect over long periods of time unless opportunities were given for responses over shorter time periods (Porter and Cleland 1995). Mini-portfolio-conferences were a way to get students to reflect when they finished a novel, a piece of writing, or a speech. These documents and discussions focused on students examining their work to determine where they were before beginning the reading, writing, or speaking; how they got to where they were; and what they needed to do next. One of our purposes was for students to determine what their individual processes were so they could tap into what worked for them during future engagements with reading, writing, or speaking. We also wanted to help students determine what they might need to do next and how we might be able to help them in their future work—discovering what skills they were demonstrating in their work and what skills they need to develop next was a part of the informative feedback that we hoped to accomplish in these conferences. The conferences could be as simple as students organizing their work, considering the reflective questions, and then sitting down to talk with us while classmates were reading and/or using the computer lab. A given conference typically culminated with setting goals for the student's next experiences (for more, see Goal-Setting Conferences in Appendix D).

What We Learned

- Since we found that reading and analyzing the core literature provided models for the types of writing that students would produce and helped them generate ideas for their writing, most of us were on similar schedules and needed the computer lab at the same time. In the past, on a traditional schedule, we had signed up for an entire period in the lab, and in our first term on the block we continued to reserve the computers in the same way. After our first experience of competing for the computer lab, however, we decided on thirty-minute time blocks for scheduling classes into the lab.

- Creating different rubrics with students for each of our classes seemed to take too much class time, especially when all of the rubrics ended up with the same criteria stated in different ways. However, we realized that this essential difference was what made the strategy work—it was the specific language that came from class discussions and found its way into the rubric that helped students to understand the characteristics of a high-quality piece and how they would be graded. After working with the strategy a few times, we discovered that once classes have created a rubric for speaking or writing, some characteristics could remain the same for future rubrics they create. For example, eye contact would always be a component of the effective delivery of a speech. When new rubrics need to be created for different forms of writing or speaking, the class can focus on specifics related to the type of work students will be creating for this particular project. Using the first rubric as a template for later rubrics saved us time and helped remind us of areas to consider in our next analysis of a type of speech or a piece of writing.

- Since our units were developed around inquiry questions and since we had selected core novels, we were able to some extent to predict questions that students would have, as well connections they might make. Providing the library and media services staff with copies of units and setting aside time for grade-level teachers to talk through the possible areas of investigation helped in ordering materials that would support the work students would be doing and in expanding print and nonprint collections.

- The value of videotaping student speeches quickly became apparent as a way to document growth over time and as a source for identifying strengths and goals that needed to be set. However, taping each student every time he or she spoke was complicated, until we developed a process that eventually involved students in taking more responsibility. When students entered their first year at MHS, they were required to bring in a blank videotape. (Our school didn't want to increase the supply fee that students were charged at the beginning of the school year.) During their English class, each student labeled the tape with his or her name and year of graduation. Teachers collected all tapes and stored them in their rooms or offices for use throughout the year. Teachers also trained students to videotape speeches during class time. At the end of the school year, rooms were set aside for organizing tapes alphabetically by year for summer storage. The following school year, they were redistributed by the teacher and instructional aide in the Advancement Center (see Chapter 7), as the student workload was fairly light at the beginning of the year. When students gave their last speech during their senior year, the tape was theirs to keep.

Writing Process Resources

Atwell, Nancie. 1987. *In the Middle: Writing, Reading, and Learning with Adolescents*. Upper Montclair, N.J.: Boynton/Cook.

Barnes, Donna, Katherine Morgan, and Karen Weinhold, eds. 1997. *Writing Process Revisited: Sharing Our Stories*. Urbana, Ill.: National Council of Teachers of English.

Daniels, Harvey, and Marilyn Bizar. 1998. *Methods That Matter: Six Structures for Best Practice Classrooms*. York, Maine: Stenhouse.

Elbow, Peter, and Pat Belanoff. 1995. *A Community of Writers: A Workshop Course in Writing*. New York: McGraw-Hill.

Murray, Donald M. 1990. *Shoptalk: Learning to Write with Writers*. Portsmouth, N.H.: Boynton/Cook.

National Writing Project materials (see http://www.writingproject.org).

Pirie, Bruce. 1997. *Reshaping High School English*. Urbana, Ill.: National Council of Teachers of English.

Ray, Katie Wood. 2001. *The Writing Workshop: Working through the Hard Parts (And They're All Hard Parts)*. Urbana, Ill.: National Council of Teachers of English.

Tchudi, Stephen, ed. 1997. *Alternatives to Grading Student Writing*. Urbana, Ill.: National Council of Teachers of English.

Weaver, Constance. 1996. *Teaching Grammar in Context*. Portsmouth, N.H.: Boynton/Cook.

Zemelman, Steven, and Harvey Daniels. 1988. *A Community of Writers: Teaching Writing in the Junior and Senior High School*. Portsmouth, N.H.: Heinemann.

5 Teaching Yearbook and Newspaper on the Block

Diane VonderHaar
Mundelein High School, Mundelein, Illinois

The purpose of journalism education is to teach students to become better writers, and the block schedule helps achieve this purpose by allowing more time for students to be involved in the writing process. Students enrolled in journalism are also responsible for producing student publications, and the block schedule helps achieve this purpose as well by allowing students to create flexible schedules and work in a "real-time" atmosphere that more accurately represents the use of time experienced by professional journalists.

Mundelein High School offers three journalism classes: Introduction to Journalism is a one-term prerequisite course to either Newspaper Journalism or Yearbook Journalism. Introduction to Journalism meets every day for an entire term, giving students one semester of elective credit, while Newspaper Journalism and Yearbook Journalism meet on an alternating schedule for the entire year, and each of these courses gives students two semesters of elective credit. Students can choose to take either Newspaper Journalism or Yearbook Journalism without taking the other, or they can take both courses together and receive credit for each. More specifically, in one week Newspaper Journalism meets during first period on Monday, Wednesday, and Friday, while Yearbook Journalism meets during first period on Tuesday and Thursday. The next week, Yearbook Journalism meets on Monday, Wednesday, and Friday, while Newspaper Journalism meets on Tuesday and Thursday. Students who need physical education credit can take one course or the other and go to gym class on the alternating days. Students who have either fulfilled their physical education requirements or waived out because of varsity sport participation may choose to have a free period or may enroll in both Newspaper Journalism and Yearbook Journalism and receive credit for both.

For a number of reasons, the Introduction to Journalism curriculum was written after our second year in the block schedule. The first reason became evident after the first year I taught Newspaper Journalism and Yearbook Journalism on the block schedule. Both journalism courses were offered to sophomores, juniors, and seniors. I had some seniors in my classes who had already been in journalism for two years, while I had other students who were new to journalistic writing. Because of the every-other-day schedule, it became difficult to teach the novice students the skills they needed to know while still producing the student publications required in these classes. The second reason the Introduction to Journalism class makes sense in the block schedule is that some students simply cannot fit the combination of journalism and physical education into their schedules for the entire year. These students were being shut out of journalism altogether because of the schedule. The Introduction to Journalism class not only teaches students the skills they need to enter the workshop environment of either Newspaper Journalism or Yearbook Journalism and begin creating publications immediately; it also offers those students who do not wish to devote more time in their schedules to journalism a chance to learn about journalistic writing.

Introduction to Journalism is a survey course. Students enrolled in the class not only learn how to interview and write news stories, feature stories, sports stories, and editorials, but also are exposed to some history and ethical considerations of journalism. The final project required in the class is a double-page spread in which students choose the theme, write the stories, choose or take the photographs, and create the layout either on a paste-up sheet or on the computer using Page-Maker 6.5. The textbook *Journalism Today* (Ferguson, Patten, and Wilson 1998) is used along with various supplementary materials.

The ninety-minute period on the block schedule facilitates this type of class quite well. On a typical day in Introduction to Journalism, I spend thirty minutes reviewing key journalistic concepts such as writing news story leads. The students then spend the next thirty minutes in small groups analyzing leads they found in a daily newspaper according to the criteria presented in the lesson, and the final thirty minutes are spent in a whole-class discussion about the effectiveness (or lack thereof) of the leads they found in the newspapers. The homework calls for the students to write five leads of their own from information found in the text.

After the criteria for writing effective stories are discussed, students then follow the writing process when creating their stories. At the beginning of a ninety-minute period, students brainstorm ideas individually for the first fifteen minutes, keeping in mind the audiences of the school newspaper and yearbook. During the next fifteen minutes, students share all their ideas as an entire class, and I write all suggestions on a large flip-chart pad. This process not only allows students to see the ideas of all the members of the class, but also often produces lively discussions that inevitably lead to additional story ideas. Immediately following the brainstorming session, students decide on the stories that interest them. It usually takes about thirty minutes for students to choose their stories. I ask all students to write their names on a small piece of paper that I place in a box. As I pick each student name out of the box, that particular student chooses his or her story topic. When all students have their topics, we move to the prewriting phase of the process.

During prewriting, students must decide the angle of the story. Students have the final thirty minutes of the period to formulate these ideas for their stories. What do they want to find out about their topic? Where do they need to go to find this information? Who do they need to interview? I require students to include at least one quote from three different people in all news, feature, and sport stories. They then must formulate the questions they want to ask these people during their interviews. Because of the ninety minutes available in the block schedule, students are able to begin formulating ideas about story topics that are fresh in their minds from brainstorming discussions. In a traditional schedule, it is often difficult for students to shift gears and remember today exactly what it was about a story that they so wanted to write yesterday. The block schedule, however, allows a logical break in this writing process as opposed to the illogical break often forced by the traditional forty-five- or fifty-minute period.

After prewriting is completed, students then set out to complete research on their topics and interview the appropriate people. We usually spend one ninety-minute period for this process. Some students go to the library to find information, some look on the Internet, and some set up interview appointments for other times during the day, or they may find administrators, teachers, coaches, or students available to be interviewed immediately. The ninety-minute block period allows students time to gather, edit, and synthesize this information in one sitting while it is still fresh in their minds.

Students then write a first draft of their stories for homework. The first draft is usually due two days after the research day. The day between the research and the due date for the first draft is usually spent looking at models of the particular type of story that the students are writing. I usually ask the students to bring in an example of the particular type of story from a newspaper, and I also supply an exemplar that students can use as a model for their own writing. During this class period, I spend approximately twenty minutes reading my exemplar aloud and discussing it with the class. The students spend the next twenty minutes in small groups reading the stories they found aloud to each other and discussing whether their stories contain effective or ineffective components of the particular type of story. We then take the last twenty minutes to discuss the stories and the components. During this time, we also discuss how the students can use the effective components to improve their own stories and decide on which ones they will use in the current stories they are writing. During the last thirty minutes of class, students work on incorporating these elements into their current rough draft. Thus the ninety-minute period allows students to read models, reflect on their effective components, and then try to incorporate those components in their own stories at one sitting, thus experiencing a writing process much like a professional journalist.

We devote the day on which the first draft is due to editing, participating in Authors' Circles and individual student/teacher conferences where we attend to content and writing issues in the stories. During this ninety-minute period, students assemble in groups of four and read each of the group members' papers. They then write comments and questions in the margins of the paper to help the author improve the paper. The students have the criteria for each story before they begin writing, and we have already discussed effective components of the particular type of story, so at this point they are able the critique and assist in the improvement of each other's stories. While students are participating in these Authors' Circles, I meet individually with each of the students to read and discuss their stories. I also ask questions, make comments, and check for spelling and grammatical errors at this time.

At this point in the process, students are often at different stages of story completion. Some students have beautiful first-draft stories that need little revision, while others might have had difficulty scheduling appointments and therefore need more content in the stories, and still others might need to make significant structural or grammatical revisions. I therefore always have an additional assignment ready for those students who have fewer revisions to make on their stories. These assignments range from writing an additional practice story based on information I provide to looking at the many other high school newspapers I receive and critiquing particular stories. The entire class is responsible for this assignment, but those who are finished can begin while the others are conferencing and revising.

After the peer editing, teacher conferences, and revisions are completed, students turn in the final drafts of their stories along with all the prewriting and drafts. I then grade the stories according to the rubric that I gave students before the writing process begins. If students turn in their final drafts on time, I allow them to revise again even after a grade has been given for each story. I have found that it sometimes takes students two and even three revisions before a story is well written, and, because one semester of Introduction to Journalism consists of a nine-week term on the block schedule, stories need to be completed in a fairly short amount of time. This revision policy gives those students who need it a little more time to perfect their stories, while the entire class moves on to another story. I also encourage students to write the best stories possible by promising to place some of them in the school newspaper. Those students who are motivated to get their name in print work diligently on their stories, and I usually have quite a few that make it into the paper.

While I use the writing process extensively, I also used the following learning/teaching strategies:

Journals: Journalists need to constantly be on the lookout for stories, and story ideas can come from many different sources, including personal experiences, observations, and experiences of friends and relatives. Students keep daily journals to record such experiences and include any story ideas they may generate each day.

Peer editing: Journalists must become comfortable with having their peers edit and revise their work. Group members edit each other's papers for content, journalistic requirements and quality, and grammar.

Authors' Circle: Revision is an important step in the writing process, and students use the Authors' Circle strategy as another way to use each other's insights in the revision of their writing. Students read each other's stories and make constructive suggestions for improvement, and the authors then take these comments into consideration when revising.

Peer coaching: Students enrolled in Newspaper Journalism who possess knowledge about journalism and exhibit strong writing and production abilities sometimes work with students enrolled in Introduction to Journalism who need additional assistance and guidance. Many of the seniors on the newspaper staff have free periods, as the block schedule allows students to schedule more courses than are required for graduation. If I have a student who has a free period during the period I teach Introduction to Journalism, he or she will come in and assist students a few times during the term.

Cooperative learning group participation: Students participate in cooperative learning groups to facilitate their learning in this class because:

1. Students enrolled in this class possess varying knowledge bases and abilities. In heterogeneous cooperative learning groups, students with more experience assist those students with less experience.

2. In cooperative learning groups, students take responsibility for their own learning and for meeting assignment deadlines. This is an important concept to grasp in this class, as the students must also take responsibility for meeting writing, editing, and production deadlines for producing a newspaper or yearbook.

3. Journalists must work together with many people to get their job done. By working in cooperative learning groups, students learn how to get along and work with their peers.

Direct Instruction: Occasional whole-class minilessons are presented by means of direct instruction to relate basic information and skills. These minilessons may include writing structure (e.g., how to write leads, the inverted-pyramid style of news writing), grammar instruction based on the needs of the students, information on group dynamics, proofreading marks, and other material as the need arises.

Role Playing: Students use role playing to explore ethical issues in journalism. Students are given a situation and asked to act out various scenarios. This teaching strategy allows students to explore various sides of an ethical issue and compare alternative views. Through this process, students better understand their own views and feelings about a particular issue, as well as those of others involved in the situation. Students discuss and debate issues such as plagiarism, confidentiality of sources, and the U.S. Supreme Court's Hazelwood decision (addressing school administrators' power to censor student media).

After students have completed the one-term prerequisite Introduction to Journalism class, they are allowed to enroll in either Newspaper Journalism or Yearbook Journalism. The Newspaper Journalism class is responsible for producing the *Mustang*, a 12-page monthly newspaper, while the Yearbook Journalism class is responsible for producing the *Obelisk*, the 208-page yearbook. Both of these classes are run as workshop classes with minilessons given as necessary. I try to give these students as much ownership as possible over the publications they produce.

In Newspaper Journalism, the editor in chief is responsible for running the brainstorming sessions that facilitate story ideas. The same system for collecting story ideas is used in this class as in Introduction to Journalism, so the students are familiar with the process. I require students to write at least three stories each month, which produces over sixty stories for possible publication in the newspaper. Students know that if they want to be published, their stories have to be exemplary.

We discuss audience frequently during brainstorming sessions. Students often poll the student body formally and informally to find out what our audience wants to read in the newspaper. Because our paper is published only once a month, we often have difficulty with timeliness. We try to take a featurized approach with most of our stories and always have to consider when the paper will be distributed when we decide what stories to write.

After students choose the stories they want to write, they usually have a week and a half to produce the first draft. When the first drafts are submitted, each section editor reads and edits all of the stories that will appear in his or her section, and I also read all of the stories and edit them before the next class period. Students then usually have another week to complete their final drafts.

The editors are then responsible for laying out the paper using PageMaker 6.5. Editors usually have one week at the most to complete the layout before we need to send the paper to the printer. The editors realize that they usually have to come to the journalism computer lab outside of class time to complete the layout. When the layout is complete, students receive computer-printed copies of the final draft of the paper and carefully read through each page to look for grammatical errors, confusing elements, and misspelled names. We then go over each page as an entire class, and the editors mark down all the errors and then go straight to the computers to fix any mistakes. The ninety-minute period facilitates this editing process in that we can all edit the paper in one period and then send the paper to the printer that afternoon.

The block schedule also creates some challenges during this process since we meet only every other day. If the layout week happens to land on a week when we meet only twice, the editors certainly have to come in either before or after school to complete their layouts. Holiday weeks also pose some difficulty because we might have two weeks in a row when we meet only twice. Because the block schedule allows students to schedule more classes than are required for graduation, most of the newspaper editors have a free period during the day, and they realize they are expected to come to the journalism lab to finish their layouts during these free periods.

While the editors are working on the layout, I usually have an alternative assignment for the rest of the class. One additional assignment involves the writing of satire, and, for the second year now, students are writing satirical stories for possible publication in a special April edition of the newspaper. Not only do we look at models of effective satire and discuss the elements of satire, but also this assignment gives the students a chance to work on some creative writing possibilities.

Because of the workshop atmosphere of this class and the importance of student responsibility for the quality of the newspaper, setting goals and evaluating progress are important aspects of the course. Students set goals and action plans for themselves at the beginning of each term relative to the aspects of journalistic writing they feel they need to improve, such as writing leads, incorporating quotes into their stories, or conducting more effective interviews. At the end of each term, students then write a reflection letter stating whether or not they have met their goals and why. They also then set new goals, or decide to continue to work on the ones they had already set, and write action plans to guide their writing improvement during the next term. I meet individually with students during the term to discuss their progress and growth.

The Yearbook Journalism class is also run in a workshop environment, and setting goals and monitoring progress are integral parts of this class as well. Minilessons are also taught on yearbook design, layout, copywriting, and PageMaker 6.5. Projects relating to yearbook production are also assigned throughout the year.

Students are given as much authority as possible over the decision-making processes in the development of the yearbook. At the beginning of the year, the entire class decides on the theme of the yearbook and the cover design. They are aware of the monetary constraints in the production process and realize that unmet deadlines, color pages, and various extras in the yearbook cost money. They also develop and participate in fund-raising efforts that allow them to incorporate the extras on their wish lists into the yearbook. In the past we have organized candy sales, car washes, and a gift-wrapping service. Assuming this kind of responsibility adds to students' ownership of the publication.

The editor in chief is responsible for overseeing the entire production of the yearbook as well as proofreading all the proofs that come back from the printing plant. Section editors are responsible for creating the layouts to be used in their sections, creating the division pages, and overseeing the completion of all the pages included in their sections before they are sent to the printing plant. The photo editor is responsible for scheduling all the photos with the photographer as well as keeping track of what photos have been received and filing them accordingly.

Students choose the pages they want to produce and are then responsible for writing all the copy, making sure photos are taken, and placing all the information on the computer layout. Deadlines are set for each stage of completion. Computer time is sometimes scarce around deadline times, especially on the weeks when Yearbook Journalism meets only twice, so students also know that if they cannot work on a computer during class time they must come to the journalism computer lab either before or after school to complete their layouts. Again, many of the yearbook staffers are seniors who often come to the journalism lab during their free periods.

Our yearbook publisher representative also comes to class a couple periods a month to assist students with the yearbook computer program, layout and cover designs, mug-shot page preparation, and various complications that arise throughout the year. The ninety-minute period facilitates her visits as we can gain more knowledge from her in fewer visits to the school.

Flexibility is key when teaching journalism on the block schedule. Most students who take Newspaper or Yearbook Journalism commit an entire period every other day to the class for the entire year as opposed to other classes that meet every day for only 18 weeks. The Introduction to Journalism class gives students an idea of what scholastic journalism is all about and helps them make an informed choice as to whether they want to pursue journalism and join the *Mustang* or *Obelisk* staff. Introduction to Journalism also allows me to recruit the most talented and dedicated writers. When students see their stories published in the school newspaper, they are usually hooked. Most students who enroll in Newspaper Journalism or Yearbook Journalism as sophomores or juniors stay in the class until they graduate. Sometimes students have to leave journalism for a term or two when they must fit another required course into their schedules, but I understand this situation and always welcome them back when they return.

Some students choose to take both Newspaper Journalism and Yearbook Journalism. I then see those students ninety minutes every day for the entire year, and I allow these students to work on either newspaper or yearbook work in each class as deadlines dictate. I also have some newspaper students who have a free period during the yearbook class and visa versa and choose to come to the class on their off days and work on their stories or other work on the computer, and this is also allowed.

The real verdict on the effectiveness of the every-other-day system of teaching journalism on the block schedule comes from the students themselves. I asked my current journalism students to share their opinions about the schedule, and I was pleased to find an overall positive attitude about the course. Here are some of their comments:

> I think that our system of block scheduling works well with journalism. Having yearbook every other day lets us have it all year. This is completely necessary! I like having it every other day because it gives you more time between classes to get things (interviews, pictures, etc.) done. Also, this allows us to have a 90-minute class that is helpful in getting everything done. In general, I don't like the block schedule, however, I think it is good for journalism. This is a compliment from me because I'm usually very negative about block scheduling.

> I like block scheduling for yearbook. You get 90 minutes to work on your pages. You get a lot done in 90 minutes. Layouts, stories, and cropped pictures are finished by the end of the period. Even though it's every other day, during your free periods you can interview people, etc. It really is a good thing.

> I think that block scheduling is a good thing, especially for yearbook. It gives you a chance to spend time on what you're doing in class and not have to stop halfway. If you're working on a layout or putting things together, you normally have enough time. Also, if you need to conduct interviews, having the hour and a half period gives you a chance to do it in class.

> I really enjoy having journalism on the block schedule. It gives you lots of time to get lots of things done, even if it is every other day. I participate in both yearbook and newspaper and the hour and a half gives us lots of precious time to finish a lot.

> I like the idea of switching journalism and physical education off every day. Switching off everyday is just like having it every day for 45 minutes. Switching off also gives me an extra day to finish writing articles or proofreading rough drafts.
> Some things that I dislike about the block journalism schedule are having an idea for an article and not being able to talk about it that day. This is the only thing I dislike about the block journalism schedule.

> Many classes can be tedious for 90 minutes a day, however, I really like the pace that the journalism program takes. It's nice to be able to talk about current events, brainstorm for ideas, and

research information all in the same day. I don't think the newspaper would be as good as it is if we didn't have the full 90 minutes. You can't get much done in 45 minutes. I like the fact that yearbook and newspaper switch off because it gives me even more time to get information for either class. It's also a good experience to switch classes every other day because it gives us an idea of what college is like.

Journalism on the block is working out really well. It's easy to change gears from newspaper to yearbook every other day. Having an hour and a half every time we meet is great. It gives you time to talk to people about your articles and it gives you lots of time to make appointments. The block also gives you lots of time to come up with ideas for stories and then write them.

Personally I enjoy having block scheduling for journalism. It gives me a great opportunity to take more time to prepare my articles. Brainstorming and the writing process become less stressful due to the fact more time is available. Being on the block schedule also gives a person more time to fully understand and ask questions rather than being hesitant to ask because of time.

I believe that the block scheduling is a good idea and that it is worthwhile for the situation. Journalism on the block allows people to be creative as well as time to rest their minds. Having journalism every other day allows people to come up with fresh ideas and not become worn out over the course of a year. I believe it is important to keep your mind fresh and not become overwhelmed. You have more time to put your ideas together during block scheduling in the hour and a half. Coming from [a school that does not have block scheduling] where they only had classes for fifty minutes, it was tough to get going. In the fifty minute classes people have a tough time accomplishing things because the periods are too short.

I think the block schedule is both good and bad for journalism. We have 90 minutes of uninterrupted time so we can have sufficient time to brainstorm and to work on stories. We can have more in-depth class discussions to talk about ideas. You can get a lot of work done in a 90-minute class period. The block schedule has a negative effect on the layout. You have to come in after class, because it's possible to only have journalism two days in a week. It also makes deadlines harder to meet because it spreads out class time. There is less time in class for peer editing and editing a draft of the newspaper.

After teaching both journalism and English on the block schedule for the past four years I have learned that time is a precious resource in schools. Students deserve the opportunity to practice using the precious time they have in school as they would in their future careers.

Professional journalists don't sit down at 8:20 A.M. one day, work on a story for forty minutes, put it aside, pick it up again the next day at 8:20 A.M., and then repeat the process every day for two weeks until it is completed. The block schedule allows students to clearly see the process of journalism in real time.

6 Teaching Theatre on the Block

Karen M. Hall
Maine Township High School East, Park Ridge, Illinois

eaching theatre on the block was a natural transition for me. For theatre teachers, ninety-minute classes aren't a foreign concept; our college acting studio classes usually lasted at least that long. We always warmed up or started with a theatre improvisation or game. We know what a twenty- or thirty-minute coaching session is like. Most of what we did in these studios can be adapted into learner-centered class-room structures. As adults, our studios were loosely structured: a warm-up here, an improvisation there, most likely followed by scene study. In this environment, we were challenged as artists but often had to make the connections ourselves between the techniques we were using in warm-ups and improvs and the work we were doing in our scenes. When moving to the block, my primary goal was to structure this gift of time in a way that could help students make meaning of their work and make connections between their work and themselves. Most of the general concepts and strategies presented earlier in this book are equally applicable to the theatre classroom, and this chapter offers specific ideas, strategies, and advice drawn from my three years of teaching theatre on the block (as discussed at the end of this chapter, I have been off the block for three years now, but the time I spent on the block continues to affect my teaching).

Examining and Revising Curriculum

I started teaching at Mundelein High School (MHS) the year before we went to the block. I was hired knowing that this transition was occur-ring, and it was one of the reasons I wanted to teach there. I had previ-ously taught longer classes at a performing arts high school and at sum-mer theatre programs. I had always found that a schedule based on fewer yet longer class periods was more productive and provided more learning opportunities for students. There was only one section of The-atre One my first year at MHS. That was the entire theatre program. With the transition to the block and the need for more electives, the Theatre

One curriculum was to be revised and a Theatre Two curriculum was to be written.

Like most theatre teachers I know, the lessons in the Theatre One and the Theatre Two curricula I taught weren't from any one textbook or any one source. They were a collection of theatre games, improvisations, projects, and scenes that I had collected and adapted over the years. One of the challenges I knew I faced was paring down the projects I used to include in my Theatre One and Theatre Two classes. Like my English colleagues, I realized that in teaching on the block I would need to use fewer assignments with more learning experiences. When I had revised these courses at my previous school, I had grouped projects into units and then wrote unit objectives to match. This time, I used the same curriculum-writing format that the English teachers were using. I found that writing course objectives followed by unit objectives and then choosing or redesigning projects for authentic assessment was an extremely effective method for restructuring these courses. I knew I was going to have to create authentic assessments that addressed a number of objectives rather than one or two objectives. Stanislavsky said it best when talking about acting: "Less is more." The same holds true when revising curriculum for the block. Through backwards planning, I realized I was going to have to give up some of the projects that I just liked to do. When I started to look at how each project fit into the core unit plan, I discovered that some of the projects I did were just a repetition of others and really didn't have any new instructional objectives.

For example, I discovered that throughout the course of a year I taught three separate projects that focused on using actions to demonstrate characters. Each project was an excellent way to address this outcome but there was little difference in the acting concepts that were addressed in each activity. I developed the following analogy for revision: the curriculum was going to have to be redesigned as a gourmet seven-course meal rather than an all-you-can-eat buffet. What I was able to do was turn some of those projects I loved into introductory activities. For instance, instead of having students do a whole scene based on animal abstraction and spending five days preparing and presenting it, I used this project as the basis of one day's warm-up. The students were still able to practice the skill of taking an animal's physical characteristics and making them part of their character. We just didn't make long improvisations about them. I kept reminding myself to think outside of the box by turning projects I loved into class warm-ups or introductory activities. I soon found that the Theatre One and Theatre Two curricula I wrote for the block were a great improvement over what I had previously taught.

Unit Structures

I usually began each unit with a number of activities or theatre games that introduced our topic. Once we got going, there were usually two or three projects tied into the unit objectives. Each project involved time for playwriting, rehearsal, a first showing, and revision and rehearsal, followed by a second showing. We always ended units by writing a final status report in our journals.

Use of Time

Block scheduling allowed me to begin class with a warm-up or theatre game related to that class's activities on almost a daily basis. After that, we moved into our topic for the day, whether it was playwriting, rehearsing, or presenting the first or second showing of a scene. We ended class by taking five or so minutes to finish up our journals for the day, either responding to a prompt or completing the critiques that we were writing during class. Altogether, it felt more like an actor's studio. There was something about spending more time per day on our art that made it feel more important. The students took their work more seriously and were able to devote more energy and effort to more meaningful scenes and projects. The additional time let me spend time coaching scenes or making connections. With fewer scenes to complete, I could spend more time helping students improve on each element of their scenes. It also let me take the time to add a quick acting exercise in the middle of class or at the end of class if it would help us to master the content.

Rehearsal Strategies

We spent at least one ninety-minute period per project rehearsing our scenes. In teaching forty-five-minute classes, I often felt frustrated during rehearsal days. Students would come into class and settle down while I would take attendance. Then I would explain what I wanted them to accomplish in rehearsal that day and send them off into their groups. Again, they needed a little time to get settled and start working. If we were lucky, this left us with twenty-five minutes to rehearse and then five minutes to come back as a group to write in our journals and debrief about what we had accomplished that day. It never seemed as if we got focused, and just when we were on a roll, it was time to stop for the day. Block scheduling changed that lack of accomplishment.

I'll admit to being nervous at first when I started having rehearsal days on the block. I expected the unfocused, frenzied feeling simply to be extended to a longer period of time. What I found however, was that the small rehearsal groups were able to accomplish so much more because they were able to focus their attention and efforts on the task at hand rather than speeding through the work with one eye on the clock. It did take the addition of rehearsal strategies, however, to keep the students focused with extended time for working in groups throughout the year. I found that giving the students a specific role or task during rehearsal time resulted in more productive sessions and increased students' learning because they were able to make specific connections between the assessment criteria and their own work. For example, a student who was struggling with creating a believable inner monologue for his or her own scene was often able to make progress after successfully describing how other students were able to create a successful inner monologue for their own scenes.

It wasn't easy. In the beginning of the year, I spent as much time teaching the students how to rehearse effectively as I did teaching them acting skills. What I discovered, however, is that the sooner I introduced a strategy that empowered the students to become directors, the sooner they became as interested in their peers' work as they were in their own work. This became a tremendous confidence builder for students who were struggling as performers. It made them feel important if they could offer feedback and give direction during a scene, even if they were struggling themselves. It also gave me an opportunity to see if a student could apply an acting concept as a director that he or she was wrestling with as a performer. Many of my weaker performers actually became some of my strongest directors. By learning some specific rehearsal techniques and strategies, the students were able to develop good habits and then were able to run their own rehearsals by the end of the year, choosing the strategy that worked best for them. Not only did this lead to a more productive classroom, it also helped me meet the Illinois Fine Arts standard in directing.

I developed each of the following strategies as a means by which to focus the students' rehearsal time when Mundelein went to block scheduling. What I discovered is that every moment of time I had with my students on the block had to be used more productively than when I taught on a traditional schedule, because the focus of each lesson had become depth rather than coverage. Going to the block forced me to be more creative in how I structured my classroom. I still use these rehearsal strategies today, even though I no longer teach on the block.

Rehearsal Strategy One

My Theatre One students almost always write a score of actions before they begin rehearsing. The following strategy helps students revise their scores as well as helps them rehearse; I find it particularly helpful when students are preparing pantomimes, in which they often tend either to forget where they have visualized objects or to "float" objects because they have forgotten to put them down. In groups of four or more, one student is the performer, one student reads the score, one student takes notes for the performer in the performer's journal, and the rest of the students serve as the director. The performer sets up all of the necessary props for the scene. The reader reads the first action out loud, and the actor then executes the action. The directors watch the action to make sure it is clear and believable. If everyone agrees that the first action is acceptable, the scene starts over. This time the reader reads the first action again, the actor executes that action, and then the reader adds the second action once the first action is complete. If everything is OK, the process is repeated adding the third action. If an action is unclear or missing, the directors take time to rehearse the actor on that particular action and the note taker writes a note to the actor in his or her journal about that moment. This way, the student has a record of what was revised as he or she rehearsed and thus can go back and revise the score by adding actions that he or she discovered had been left out or by deleting actions unnecessary to the story.

This strategy allows the student actors to focus on what they are doing in the moment. They don't have to try to remember what is next because that is someone else's job. They get feedback and suggestions on each action. They also get a chance to learn that rehearsal is about repetition as well as stopping and correcting what does not work right away, so they don't master sloppy actions or leave out important actions. It is also a chance for students to improve their observation and directing skills. This strategy is extremely helpful for novice students who are working on short nonverbal scenes. Because we divide our scenes into a beginning, middle, and end, once we have finished rehearsing the beginning section, we stop rehearsing that section and work only through the middle section. Once both sections are complete, we run the pantomime once from the beginning. Then we work on the end section. Finally, we put all of the sections together.

Beginning nonverbal scenes tend to be short, only twenty to thirty actions long in total. Each scene is usually rehearsed in fifteen minutes, and the group can finish looking at everyone's scenes in about sixty minutes. The teacher's role becomes that of facilitator. Because I will be coaching the performer's scene later, I spend my time going from group to group working with the directors, note takers, and readers, giving them suggestions on how they can be more effective in their roles. I also remind them that part of their job is to let the actors know what they are doing well as they are doing it.

Rehearsal Strategy Two

Another group rehearsal strategy is to appoint specific roles to each member of the group. Again, the students are working in groups of four. While one student is rehearsing a scene, the others are serving as student directors. For each rehearsal, a given student director looks only for one specific element and works on that element with the performer— for example, tempo-rhythm, transitions, blocking, nonverbal actions, verbal actions, characterization, intentions, and obstacles. I assign these topics to the directors based on the elements of the scene that the student actors are focusing on. Students can either take notes as the scene progresses or stop performers when there is something that needs to be worked on. Student directors need to be reminded to give feedback that also describes what was working in the scene as well as what could still be improved.

Rehearsal Strategy Three

Like the strategy above, this strategy breaks the scene down into its core components. The class is broken into small groups, and each group works through each of its members' scenes. As before, each scene is rehearsed multiple times. This time, however, all of the student directors focus on one element of the scene together. The first time through the scene, the only element that might be worked on is tempo-rhythm, the second time through it might be blocking, the third time through it might be characterization, and so on. This approach helps the student directors master their observation skills and their directing skills.

Rehearsal Strategy Four

I started using this strategy, called Rehearsal Circles, when I saw how effective Authors' Circles were in English classes. We use virtually the same critique form that the English students use, slightly altered for a theatre classroom: Students watch their classmates rehearse a scene and then provide feedback about what was done well and ask questions about portions of the scene that were unclear. It was an easy transition for the students once they had worked on Authors' Circles in their other classes, and it was a great opportunity to demonstrate to students how a learning strategy in one class could be applied to another class.

Rehearsal Strategy Five

For second showings, the strategy I usually implement is Rehearsing for Goals. Students set their goals for improvement individually based on the feedback they received from their first showing. Three to five specific goals are usually appropriate. Once the goals are set, students break into small groups for rehearsal. The student actor explains his or her performance goals to the group and then performs the scene for feedback. Students are to focus their critiques on helping the actor achieve his or her goals.

Journal Strategies

Being on the block gave each class more time to be reflective, and I found this to be one of the greatest benefits of the block schedule. Reflection allows students to work their way through the connections they need to make in order to understand and master each acting technique they cover in class. Because they were writing ninety entries instead of one hundred eighty entries, the writing became more focused. They weren't writing on the same prompt for six or seven days straight. I also began to enjoy reading journals more because I was able to give prompts that promoted higher levels of critical thinking. I was getting to know my students better. I also had less reading to do. I used to collect seventy-five notebooks eight times a year, and every time I collected a notebook there were about twenty entries. That was fifteen hundred entries I had to read eight times a year for a grand total of twelve thousand entries. On the block, I collected notebooks only four times over the course of eighteen weeks. Already, this reduced by half the number of entries that I had before going to the block. Granted, these entries were longer, but they also had more meaning and more information, and thus they were more valuable for me as an evaluator and for the student. As described above in the section on rehearsal strategies and below in the section on scene presentation strategies, I incorporated journal writing into these activities. I also made it a point to try to give a specific writing prompt at the end of class every day. We would take at least five minutes at the end of class to answer this prompt as a way of constructing meaning for ourselves based on our classroom activities that day.

Scene Presentation Strategies

Looking at six scenes or seven scenes a day can be tough for students. My priority is always to keep the way we do coachings fresh and to vary the students' responsibilities as we give feedback in order to keep the class focused. In every situation, there is some journal entry that needs to be made. Here are some different ways I have handled this process.

First Showings

During first showings, the actor performs the scene and then the class and the teacher give the performer feedback through an oral critique session. We also go back and work on some of the sections of the scene that need the most improvement.

The hardest part is for students to sit in the audience and take notes in their notebooks and stay focused on each scene. One thing I try to do is move through the space while critiquing scenes. Also, I try to make some connections between the scene we are working on and other work we have already seen. One thing we never do is to watch the six or seven scenes straight through; we always take a brief intermission at the halfway point.

Students participate in this process by offering comments and by writing critiques in their journals. I use the following journal/oral feedback strategies to vary the focus of the critique sessions. These are just a few of the different ways I try to create variety in the critique sessions during first showings.

1. Two Keepers and an Upgrade: Ask students to pick out two elements of the scene that were well done and should be "keepers" for the second showing. Make sure they describe why each is a "keeper." Ask students also to pick out one element that needs to be "upgraded" for the second showing and have them explain how they would direct that element.

2. Make Connections: Ask students to watch each scene and then make a connection between the scenes they are watching and their own scene. Are there pointers they could pick up and apply to their own work? Have students share these with the class as part of the critique session.

3. Be the Expert: Ask students to focus on one element of the scene. They will be asked to share their comments about that element during the critique with the performer. Each day, I assign different students different elements to critique. This is

an excellent way to help students strengthen their ability to define and describe specific components of the acting process.

4. Critique the Teacher: Here the students get to do just that—critique the teacher's critique. The students take notes on the coaching process. Do they agree or disagree with the suggestions I have given? What would they have done differently? Their portion of the critique session then focuses on sharing those observations with the class.

5. Jigsaw Coachings: I use this strategy when we are working on scenes or monologues and multiple students are performing the same piece. Each person who is performing the same piece presents his or her first showing on the same day. Instead of coaching the entire monologue or scene for each performer, I coach only a section of the piece in greater depth for each person. Then I coach the next section with the next performer. That way, we don't have to watch the same piece over and over and the students get to apply their observations from another scene to their own work.

Second Showings

These showings tend to go much more quickly; in fact, we usually do them in two days. Each student sets up, shares what he or she worked on between the first and second showing, and then performs his or her scene. Then we move on to the next scene. The students who are observing use their journals to take notes for each scene. We always debrief when we are done with a group of six performers. I use two different strategies for these sessions, panel discussion and round robin.

Panel Discussions

In this format, once all of the students in the group have finished their scenes they all sit onstage with their notebooks and we have a panel critique session. We talk about each person in the group, trying to get four or five comments for each of them. The focus usually is on what improved since the first showing and how well each actor achieved his or her goals for this scene. The student performers are also allowed to ask questions if they want specific information about a moment in their scene. Each performer is instructed to take notes about the feedback he or she receives.

Round Robin

The observers are divided into three or four groups and move to different places in the room. The performers are also divided among these groups. Each group gets about five minutes to debrief with the performers, and then the performers switch groups for another debriefing session. This continues until the performers have visited every group. The teacher can either join a group or move from group to group to keep the critiques focused.

Performance Portfolios

With the implementation of block scheduling, I also began implementing a voice and movement portfolio in my Theatre One class. This unit was always particularly difficult when I was teaching forty-five-minute periods. Voice and movement is a very scary process for most teenagers. It involves risk taking in front of one's peers and focusing on some very difficult techniques that are developed only through much repetition, such as physical alignment and vocal production. I always felt that it was necessary to warm up or do some type of voice-and-movement activity at the beginning of every class. We also had four different projects to complete: a staged choral reading with the entire class, a staged short poem in small groups, a haiku movement improvisation, and a solo oral interpretation. For the students, this became a very tedious, time-consuming process. On the block, however, I was able to more efficiently use the classroom time and was also able to do the projects concurrently instead of consecutively, which was how the voice-and-movement portfolio came about.

By dividing the class into segments, we could begin with a physical and vocal warm-up, move into working on one of the projects for about thirty minutes, and then spend the last thirty minutes on another project. At the end of the unit, each group had almost a twenty-minute performance to present to the class. Each group programmed its own presentation and decided on its running order. Groups also staged their transitions between pieces and tried to come up with some means of unifying their presentation. The end product was a definite improvement over the types of work the students used to present.

Technical Theatre

After the first year on the block, it became apparent that additional courses were needed in order to provide more choices for electives. Because of the 4×4 block, students who were previously enrolled in six courses in a traditional schedule all of a sudden needed to be taking eight courses. Additional electives were needed in order to provide students with enough options for their block schedule. We decided to add a course in Technical Theatre, and this elective really took off. We were always enrolled to our limits. Even when my teaching load increased from five classes on the traditional schedule to six classes on the block, we were turning students away.

This course addition not only provided a new elective for students, it also provided me with the labor I so desperately needed to complete the technical elements for our theatre season. The first nine weeks of the course focused on set construction. We were able to learn all of the basic skills of construction and painting and then apply them to practical projects that helped build the sets for either the fall play or the winter musical. Students were able to make important contributions to our productions. I was very careful to keep the Technical Theatre students' contributions separate from that of the technicians working in the extracurricular program; that way they could take a project from start to finish and feel ownership about what they had done.

As you may well imagine, having ninety minutes a day to work on set construction is much more effective than trying to set up, do work, and then clean up for an afternoon rehearsal in forty-five minutes. During the second nine weeks of the course, we were more project-based. We focused on lighting, props, costumes, sound, and stage management. The ninety-minute classes allowed us to spend quality time completing a project, rather than getting something out, working on it briefly, and then having to clean it up again for the night.

Nuts and Bolts

Space is one of the greatest luxuries I had when we went to block scheduling. I didn't teach in a classroom—I taught in the auditorium and also used my attached shop space. When we broke into small groups, the groups could work far enough away from each other that they weren't distracted by each other. On the rare occasions when we had to move out of the auditorium and into our small dressing rooms or acting studio area on a rehearsal day, we were never able to get as much work accomplished.

The only element of scheduling that I found to be important was that the two sections of Technical Theatre needed to be run in different terms so that I had a yearlong labor force. Also, I made sure that Technical Theatre was scheduled during the last period of the day. This allowed us to leave incomplete scenic elements out on stage to dry without the fear of an acting class coming in and having to put things away so that class could be taught. We were always able to move after-school rehearsals to another space if necessary, but we never had a truly satisfactory alternative space to use during the school day.

Leaving the Block

I've been "off the block" now for three years, and what I miss most is having ninety minutes of consecutive instructional time. Having taught for three years on the block, I found it especially frustrating to go back to forty-two-minute classes. All of the approaches I had used to structure lessons over ninety minutes in order to help my students construct meaning were now more difficult to implement. During my first year off the block, I went back into a buffet-style curriculum with lots of projects, even more than I used to teach before I revised the curriculum for our transition to block scheduling. While I have been successful in paring down the amount of coverage, I can no longer start every class period with a warm-up or introductory activity, because it isn't practical. Again, it seems that rehearsals just get started and the bell rings. It also seems to take forever to finish first and second showings of a scene.

The most striking observation I have made is that fewer students in this format have been as successful in developing the analytical skills that my students on the block were able to develop. Without those skills, students aren't developing their technique as quickly or as deeply as my students did on the block. Their critiques aren't as focused or as accurate. Their journal entries aren't quite as detailed. They never really develop as strong a rehearsal ethic as the students at Mundelein did. We cover more material, but the curriculum sacrifices the depth to which we covered the objectives on the block schedule. The talented students are able to grow on their own in this process, but I never feel that the students who need help discovering and developing their technique really get a fair chance. Due to the current schedule, I have limited time to structure activities that help students create more significant meaning and better connections.

Nonetheless, I am able to use the lessons I learned while teaching on the block. I still use all of the rehearsal strategies, journal strategies, and scene presentation strategies that have been discussed throughout this chapter. Being on the block forced me to look at teaching from a new vantage point. Through that experience I know I have become a more effective and creative teacher. The lessons I learned during those three years will continue to shape and inform the ways I design and implement curricula in any kind of schedule.

7 Considering Other Instructional and Departmental Changes

Carol Porter
National-Louis University, Chicago, Illinois
Deerfield High School, Deerfield, Illinois

Diane VonderHaar
Mundelein High School, Mundelein, Illinois

Offering More Electives

On the block schedule, students have the opportunity to take more classes, and in some schools this boosts the enrollment in many of the electives that are already being offered. At Mundelein High School (MHS), we had many courses "on the books" that students had not signed up for over the years as graduation requirements had increased in other content areas. We considered bringing these electives back into existence but discovered that many were developed around the interests and talents of a particular teacher, in most cases one who was no longer teaching in our school. We had also revised so much of our curriculum that we thought the needs of our students might be different from what they had been ten years before, so we decided to ask the students what classes they would be interested in taking. We invited students to bring their lunches into a room across from the cafeteria during their lunch periods and offered cookies and pop as an incentive to meet with us.

Our conversations with students helped us understand that, while they got touches of mythology in some of their courses, they wanted a whole course on mythology so they could study it in depth. A mythology course was planned over the next year. Students also said they wanted a course on Shakespeare but agreed that the enrollment might be limited. This led to brainstorming about other topics and authors they would like to study. Their discussion led to the ideas we put into place for two courses, one titled Expressions: Literature and the Arts and the other titled simply Senior Project. (See sample Expressions unit in Appendix F.) During these lunch meetings, students complained that the types of writing required in their first-year, sophomore, and junior English classes didn't give them the opportunity to be very creative. This suggestion led to the revision of a creative writing course that hadn't been taught in many years. All of these courses were planned over the next school year, and curriculum was written in teams during the summer. After two years, we went to the students again for feedback so that we could make revisions in the new courses and get suggestions for other courses.

What We Learned

- Enrollment was low in many of the electives the first time they were offered. When we took a closer look, we discovered that students who had suggested and enthusiastically given us ideas for courses had not signed up for them. When we asked, we found that students were not aware, and/or counselors were not sure, that the new courses would fit with students' career and educational plans. Once we began to work with counselors by explaining what each of the courses had to offer, more students signed up. The following school year, we also took time during our English classes prior to student registration to meet with each student to develop an English coursework plan. Suggestions based upon interests and talents were recorded so that students could share our recommendations with their parents and counselors.

- Because the block schedule creates the need for more electives, courses that are developed need to be teachable by several people in the department. Eliminating a course from department offerings because a teacher is no longer in the department or building creates scheduling problems on the traditional schedule, but there are even more implications on the block, such as overloading in some electives, loss of departmental FTEs or other staff positions, students being unable to get electives needed for graduation. In addition, budgeting for new electives and finding teachers to develop and write new course curriculum during the summer is often difficult, so developing new courses because someone leaves the department is a resource issue in terms of teacher time and budget (see discussion of credit requirements in Appendix B).

- On the block schedule most electives are one-semester (or one-term) offerings. Scheduling a teacher to teach an elective thus requires that he or she teach two electives; a full-year course is eliminated as a possibility as soon as a one-term course is assigned to a teacher. In the sample shown in Figure 4, if the enrollment in creative writing is limited to one section, the teacher

	Term 1	Term 2	Term 3	Term 4
Period 1	English 1	English 1	English 3	English 3
Period 2	English 3	English 3	Plan	Plan
Period 3	Plan	Plan	English 1	English 1
Period 4	Creative Writing	Senior Project	English 3	English 3

Figure 4. Sample teacher schedule with electives (each term occupies nine weeks).

needs to be able to teach one of the other semester (one-term) offerings during the second term.

- In our state, a course must meet certain criteria to be considered an English credit. For example, students enrolled in newspaper and yearbook do not receive an English credit; they receive an elective credit. It is possible for students to enroll in several elective credit courses but not have enough English credits at some universities. When expanding course offerings on the block schedule, getting necessary approval from the state or from universities, or specifying which courses are "elective credit only," will prevent problems for students.

Scheduling Advanced Placement Classes

AP classes on the traditional schedule are usually full-year courses in most schools. On the 4×4 block schedule, this presents a problem, since full-year classes usually run either through Terms 1 and 2 (September through January) or Terms 3 and 4 (January through June). To schedule this course early in the year left more than a three-month gap between the end of the course and the AP test. Scheduling the class during the second half of the year gave students only three months of classroom instruction prior to the test. We decided that the best option would be to offer AP classes for the first 3 terms of the school year (September through April), increase the credits earned to 1.5, and offer review sessions in the two to three weeks leading up to the exam during the scheduled all-school make-up time.

Using the Advancement Center for Student Support

When we first detracked English classes, we developed a course for "at-risk" students to support their transition into detracked English classes. This was our version of a Title I class, and we called it Language Arts Lab. Curriculum was written that aligned with the work students were doing in their English classes. Students earned 0.5 elective credits for the course and were identified as needing Title I support through the evaluation of a writing sample which each incoming eighth grader or transfer student wrote in response to a short story. English teachers also recommended students who were not identified by this process when they were found to be struggling in their English class.

As successful as this course was, we knew that with the move to the block schedule we would have to take another approach. To continue with this requirement on the block would have meant that identified students would be in English and English-related classes for two ninety-minute class periods, or three hours, each day. Since English class is typically the least favorite for these students, we did not think this was a wise plan.

Although we originally envisioned the Advancement Center as a support for those students who would no longer receive support from Language Arts Lab classes, we didn't want this classroom or area of the building to become labeled as a place for "dummies," nor did we think the enrichment we hoped to offer should be limited to only a few selected students. In planning the structures and materials for the Advancement Center, then, we kept our purpose in mind—support, enrichment, and advancement for all students. This was when we realized that the writing center concept could be expanded to a center that assisted students in all aspects of their learning in the English classroom.

In order to create this environment, we decided to staff the Advancement Center during each period of the school day with a full-time instructional aide and an English teacher. The aide was responsible for scheduling caseload students (students who would have enrolled in a Language Arts Lab/Title I class on a traditional schedule), maintaining and retrieving student portfolios and videos (each student had a video on which all of his or her speeches were recorded), and performing the general clerical duties associated with the functions of the Advancement Center, as well as working with students when necessary. The English teacher assigned to the Advancement Center worked with students.

We didn't want the Advancement Center to become a place where classroom teachers would send students because of classroom behavior problems, so a Student Admittance/Activity Sheet was developed to ensure that all students attending the Advancement Center would have a specific purpose for being there (see Appendix G). We also wanted to supply the Advancement Center teacher with all the resources necessary to best support student achievement. When writing the Advancement Center curriculum, we outlined all the available resources for each grade level. For example, an English teacher assigned to the Advancement Center might have taught only first-year and sophomore English, but when junior students were looking for enrichment materials to enhance their understanding of a unit, the Advancement Center teacher needed to have the curriculum document to guide students to the appropriate materials.

The Advancement Center was a way for us to maintain high expectations for students needing enrichment activities and materials after completing the core curriculum provided in their classrooms, something teachers rarely had enough time to provide during the traditional eight-period schedule. Additionally, the small group work, discussions, individual research, and group projects that have been suggested as instructional strategies for block scheduling were facilitated by the Advancement Center. For example, while the classroom teacher is conducting portfolio conferences or teaching a grammar minilesson to a small group of students (as suggested in Chapter 4), the advancement center teacher could be helping other students in the same class find resources for inquiry projects, set goals, or view videotapes of speeches.

The Advancement Center offered students the opportunity not only to seek assistance in areas of reading, writing, and speaking, but also to explore topics of interest and research related to units of study in each English course. Learning centers throughout the room contained materials relating to the unit research questions at each grade level, as well as topics encountered in core reading, writing, and speaking assignments. These materials spanned various time periods, from current events to historical documents, and encompassed a variety of communication formats, including novels, short stories, poetry, plays, newspaper and magazine articles, video- and audiotapes, posters, charts and graphs, artwork, music, and computer programs. In addition, televisions, videocassette players, audiocassette players, and video cameras were available for students to use; paperback books were available for students to check out as free-choice novels; computers were available for students to work on assignments; and areas and rooms were set up for students to work individually, with other students, and with teachers. Sample pieces of core writing and speaking assignments were also available for students to analyze prior to completing their own work.

In general, the first thirty minutes of each period was reserved for the Advancement Center teacher to meet with specific caseload students. By setting this time aside for meetings with identified students on a regular basis and tracking their progress, we were able to use Title

I money to cover some of the cost of staffing the center. At the beginning of each term, the Title I student list was reviewed and sorted by the period in which each student attended his or her English class. Meeting times were coordinated between the Advancement Center teacher, the Advancement Center aide, classroom teachers, and students. A master schedule was prepared and sent to teachers to remind them when students needed to attend their regular meetings.

Caseload students came to the Advancement Center with their Weekly Progress Sheet filled out so that the Advancement Center teacher knew exactly what skills the students were working to improve (see sample in Appendix G). Classroom teachers were also asked to fill out Student Progress Information forms each term to inform the Advancement Center teacher of the progress of each caseload student (see sample in Appendix G). These forms helped facilitate communication between the classroom teacher and the Advancement Center teacher in order to provide the best possible assistance for each student.

During the last sixty minutes of each ninety-minute class period, students needing assistance in the Advancement Center could attend with the permission of their English teacher. Students signed up to work in the Advancement Center (or their teacher signed them up) at least one day in advance of attendance. Other students were admitted on a drop-in basis during the last sixty minutes of each period, depending upon the nature of their attendance and availability of various working stations in the room. Students were required to fill out an Advancement Center Student Admittance/Activity Sheet which the classroom teacher signed prior to students leaving their regular classroom (see Appendix G). This form served both as the student's hall pass and as a means of communication between the classroom teacher and the Advancement Center teacher. The average time a student spent in the Advancement Center in any given class period was approximately thirty minutes.

Teachers assigned to the Advancement Center facilitated a variety of instructional activities, including:

- videotaping small-group discussions,
- planning group projects and presentations,
- providing feedback for oral presentations,
- viewing videos of speeches and discussions and assisting in goal setting,
- running additional and/or make-up Authors' Circles,

- supporting and editing writing in progress,
- guiding particular assignments and research and enrichment activities,
- contacting resources for and with students,
- co-teaching classes with classroom teachers when needed for special activities,
- assisting students in setting goals for reading and writing and creating action plans to attain goals (see sample forms in Appendix D),
- assisting students in skill building.

On a typical day in the Advancement Center, a group of students whose class is working on the revision aspect of the writing process could be sharing their personal narratives in an Authors' Circle to receive peer feedback for revisions. The Advancement Center teacher might be working with a caseload student who needs an editing conference to check for mechanical and grammatical errors in his or her character analysis. Five students could be using the computers to type the final drafts of their research papers, while another student might be using a computer to do Internet research. A group of three students who gave speeches in class on the previous day might be watching their videotapes to critique themselves and set speaking goals for future presentations. At the learning centers, two students who have already completed their classroom writing assignments might be reading from a packet of poetry, while three others analyze song lyrics related to the theme of their unit. (Centers are described in the next section of this chapter. See sample centers in Appendix H.)

Because the block schedule allows teachers to use additional class time for students to participate in sustained silent reading, literature circles, editing conferences, Authors' Circles, and writing workshops, the Advancement Center provides a resource, both in personnel and in physical space, to facilitate these activities. A teacher can send two groups of students to the Advancement Center to participate in Authors' Circles with help from the Advancement Center teacher, while three other groups are participating in the same activity in the classroom. Likewise, during editing conferences, the classroom teacher can meet individually with half of the students in the classroom, while the other half meet with the Advancement Center teacher. This approach allows for twice as many conferences in the same amount of class time.

More specifically, in relation to a lesson on the block schedule (e.g., see the sample class plan for literature study in Appendix C), a teacher could make arrangements for six students who were struggling to understand the required novel to go to the Advancement Center. One of the English teachers assigned to the center could read the chapter aloud to the students and use the Say Something strategy (see description in Appendix D) at various points in the text. This approach could also be used with an audiotape of the book. The Advancement Center teacher could then have these students write in their journals before they return to class in time for the literature discussion. During this same time, several students in the same class who had read ahead, and had already written in their journals before coming to class, could get a pass from their English teacher to go to the Advancement Center to work at one of several centers that had been created for the book. These students could also return to the classroom in time for discussion.

With the second class plan presented in Appendix C, for writing instruction, several students who needed assistance with incorporating information from literary criticisms into their essays could go to the Advancement Center for help during the time when the rest of the class was revising rough drafts. They might stay in the Advancement Center to use the computers available there and then return to class for Authors' Circles. Another group of students in the same English teacher's class could be scheduled for the Advancement Center so that one of the teachers there could work directly with them on a specific assignment. This work session in the Advancement Center could have been scheduled after discovering that these particular students needed help in using supporting evidence from the text for the generalizations they were making in their writing. These students could get help during the last forty-five minutes of the class period while their classmates are engaged in Authors' Circles and in making revisions in their rough drafts.

What We Learned

- This type of "loose" plan, and the philosophy that guides it, need to be approved by the administration and possibly the school board. Since the Advancement Center is not a "class" in a traditional sense, a shift to this approach—as compared with the traditional approach of scheduling students into a Title I class, where staffing needs are determined by class counts—reduces the number of teachers needed to teach specific classes. As a result, if the educational value of such an arrangement is not agreed upon by key parties, then there is a danger that changing the way we provide for student needs may be seen, in later years, primarily as a way to reduce staff (and essential programs).

Learning Centers

Learning centers are planned learning experiences that give students the opportunity to explore and extend topics of study, make choices, and work independently (Burke 1984). In many ways, learning centers are similar to the experimental stations that science teachers set up for their students, where each station offers a problem or idea to explore. In the English language arts classroom, learning centers can be created to explore the various themes and questions that emerge from a unit of study or a novel the class is reading. They can also be set up to help students further refine skills needed to achieve specific objectives. For example, centers could support the teaching of grammar in context and introduce topics of study such as story structures and the author's craft.

Personalizing instruction to meet the needs of individual learners is difficult when there are twenty-five to thirty, or more, students in a class. For example, creating a grammar lesson for a small group of students based upon an analysis of their writing is difficult when there can be as many as twenty other students who need something to do while the teacher is working with the small group. Often, teachers assign a reading for the remaining students, but there are always those students who finish early or others who can't concentrate while the "I'm finished with everything" activities of classmates are taking place around them. And then there are also the students working in the small group: when do they make up the reading that other students are doing while they are working with the teacher?

Learning centers offer the teacher and students several options for the work they will do. For example, when we needed to hold conferences with students about their writing, we might be working with five to seven students during a class period, while another five to seven were in the library or Advancement Center searching for books and/or doing research. Another small group might be reading or writing, and more small groups would be working at centers in our classroom. We could rotate students through these activities throughout the week until we had met with each student.

Making learning centers available in the classroom also provides a way for teachers to meet the demands that block scheduling makes for flexibility and variation in the instructional methods offered within a class period. While teaching on the block schedule, we could set up the rotation described above during a single class period by having students rotate every thirty minutes from small-group direct instruction, to media center/computer lab work, to learning center activities.

Centers can be arranged on tables around the classroom, but they might also be set up in special locations in the school media center and/ or in writing or tutoring areas. Learning centers might also be developed and shared by teams of teachers. At Mundelein, teachers developed learning centers to support the units they were teaching, and these centers were set up in the Advancement Center so that all students could use them.

Some centers can be set up for a short engagement in the topic, while others may require the students to return several times throughout the unit, semester, or year in order to complete the center. Still other centers, such as grammar centers, might be available throughout the year but used only as needed.

Students can also create a center for other students as a way to express and demonstrate their understanding of specific topics. Not only does such a project provide an authentic audience, but also it puts students in the role of considering how they might teach what they have learned to someone else. Centers can also be a culminating project for an area of inquiry that learners have explored. After reading the book *Night* (Wiesel 1960), for example, students in one class identified questions they had about the Holocaust, engaged in research, and created centers related to their investigations. For several days, these centers were visited by other students in the class, and they were later used by subsequent classes taught by other teachers.

8 Reflecting on Practice: What We've Learned

In preparing the manuscript for this book, we returned to many of the folders of documents we produced at Mundelein High School prior to going to the block schedule and during our first year on the block. One Communication Arts memo titled "Block Schedule Issues" had a subtitle which stated, "We feel like gerbils on a wheel." As much as we planned, as much as we prepared for every anticipated change that we thought deserved consideration, there were still issues we hadn't considered. In spite of this, we could see that the positive aspects in terms of students' learning and the type of instruction we were finally able to put in place far outweighed the problems. The memo documenting our first term on the block schedule identified several of the following unanticipated problem areas, along with changes we made to help solve the difficulties we were facing.

End-of-Term Issues

On the 4×4 block schedule, there are four terms, each of which is the equivalent of a semester on the traditional schedule. At the end of each term (every nine weeks) at Mundelein, final exams were scheduled. What we discovered was that the time previously built in for grading and preparing for new courses, in particular the 0.5-credit or one-term classes, was not built into the final exam schedule when we went to the block. During our first year on the block, we even had Homecoming during the week of final exams. Since all extracurricular activities were running on full schedule rather than the limited-activity and abbreviated-practice schedule that was usually implemented during finals week on the traditional schedule, students were less prepared and lacked focus.

In the past, most teachers had used a portion of their winter break to grade final exams, calculate grades, revise curriculum, and prepare for new courses. On the block schedule, it's possible that exams will take place on a Tuesday and Wednesday and that the new term will start on a Thursday, which is what happened to us in our first year.

What We Learned

- Some backward planning needs to be done when determining

the master schedule, so that exams can take place on a Wednesday and Thursday with a professional day built in on a Friday and new terms beginning on a Monday.

- Some scheduled events that are on the calendar before the decision to move to block scheduling may need to be changed in order to better facilitate such school-day events as final exams.

- At Mundelein, many teachers (especially teachers of one-term classes) tried giving the final exam prior to the scheduled time and then using final exam time to provide closure, discuss grades, and return papers. The problem with this plan when we first went to the block schedule was that many students weren't ready for the final, because teachers had miscalculated the time needed to do "everything" in the units. Describing the last few days of the term as a "wild scramble" for both students and teachers would be an understatement. As we became more accustomed to the block, however, this method worked.

- One plan for instruction that seemed to be a good option was to schedule speeches during final exam time. Since final exam time was never longer than a regular ninety-minute class period on the block, exam periods were no longer than any other day of the term. In order to gain a few extra days of grading time, many teachers scheduled the written portion of the exam during a class period prior to the "official" exam time and then spent the last several days with students preparing and presenting speeches. Not only were speeches much easier to grade, but also they created a sense of celebration of learning at the end of the grading period.

Scheduling

Many scheduling problems can arise when going to the block, but one we hadn't anticipated which was critical to the teaching of English wasn't discovered until well into our first month of school. The computer hadn't scheduled all students for consecutive terms! This meant that some students had English during Term 1 (from August through October) and the second half of their English class during Term 4 (April through June) of their 4×4 schedule. With this type of a switch, there was often little consistency in teachers. And, as if this weren't bad enough, we found out that some students were scheduled for the second half of their "year long" English classes before the first half!

What We Learned

- Working with counselors and the person or people in charge of scheduling and/or computer programming is more important than we realized. Even though we thought it should go without saying, we put it in writing that one-year courses should not be divided; students were required to be in consecutive terms and they had to be in the first term of the sequence before the second term of the sequence. We also required that students be scheduled for the entire year with one teacher. We could easily check this at the beginning of the school year for half of the student body by asking to see student schedules on the first day of class.

Progress Reports

One change we *didn't* make when we moved from a traditional to a block schedule was that we decided to continue filling out progress reports nearly halfway through the grading period, at four weeks. We discovered, however, that, given the need for two to three days for scheduling changes at the beginning of the term, a couple of weeks for adjustment to routines, several weeks for students and teacher to get to know one another, and two to three days prior to mailing for filling out reports, there was limited time in which to make an accurate assessment. We found that a simple solution was to wait another week before filling out progress reports. (See further discussion of progress reports in Appendix B.)

Student/Paper Load

On the 4×4 block, we were teaching approximately seventy-five students a day, and, because of the longer class periods, students were producing much more work in a single day than they had been before block. If students were completing two assignments during each class period, the teacher had approximately 150 pieces of grading to do each day. Much of the work students were turning in on one day needed to be returned to them on the following day in order for them to continue with the next lesson. When looking at a class period on the block as two class periods on a regular schedule, not returning papers to students on the next day meant students weren't getting feedback for two days.

What We Learned

- The new methods we found ourselves using—research; collaboration on projects; time for reading, writing, and revising; literature discussion; using the Advancement center; and incorporating the use of learning centers—gave us time to conference with students rather than grade. This reduced grading time considerably. For example, grading a portfolio might take twenty to thirty minutes in the evening at the kitchen table but only ten minutes during a one-on-one conference with a student.

- At one of our curriculum feedback sessions with students, they told us that we valued their opinions and ideas if they recorded them on paper but that we didn't seem to value what they had to say aloud. Guilty as charged! This caused us to reexamine our assignments and assessments and work toward balancing them. Much of what we were assessing in written assignments could, with some alterations, be done in other formats. What we didn't realize immediately was that the students' suggestion would reduce also our paper load dramatically.

- English teachers are often told to stagger the assignments between classes as a solution to the overload of paperwork that they face. The effort required to do this in terms of planning and preparation on a traditional schedule often takes as much time as grading the papers—little extra time is gained. On the block schedule, teachers become more experienced with and efficient at changing instruction, so there is more time gained if class planning considers a staggering of due dates.

Gathering Data

In our first year on the block—and with some teachers, this continued beyond the first year, whenever something went wrong—the block schedule was blamed. And there were just as many other times when things were going well that we couldn't account for the reason. The scheduling problem we ran into with students having two different teachers or inconsecutive terms of English was blamed on the block, but it was actually a computer problem. Overloading in some classes and small numbers in other classes was also blamed on the block schedule, until the principal suggested that department chairs examine the problem areas together. It was then discovered that the class periods of several new AP classes had caused the problem—a problem that would have existed on the traditional schedule if we had still been on it. Meanwhile, general attendance had improved, and many teachers attributed this to the new attendance policy, which they had been requesting for years. But how did we know the improvement wasn't due to the new instructional methods that were better matched to how students learn, and/or to the new assessments we were using, which were authentic, challenging, and meaningful?

What We Learned

- Whatever reasons have guided the decision to move to block scheduling should be considered and data should be collected.

Determining what baseline data will be gathered, who will gather it, and who will be responsible for analyzing it is crucial to determining what block scheduling revisions need to be made. These data-gathering decisions need to be made before going to the block schedule; otherwise, important pieces of information or even the opportunities to collect the data will be lost.

Determining a Revision Plan

Most schools will need to reexamine their make-up schedule several times before they figure out the times and procedures that work for them. Once the schedule for make-up time has been established, the committee should agree to meet again a time or two during the first year on the block to do some tweaking, and then again at the end of the year to consider a revision plan.

If the curriculum wasn't revised prior to block scheduling, this will be an important task after the first year on the block, since much of the instruction will have changed over the school year.

Each block-schedule decision-making committee (see Chapter 1) might reconvene halfway through the first year on the block to consider how their decisions are working in practice. Having committee members get feedback from each department is crucial to this process, and one important area of discussion for each committee involves considering whether or not decisions have had enough time to work.

Continuing to Work with Parent Groups

It's interesting how quickly doing something new comes to seem common. In some respects, that's a reassuring thought—adapting to a new teaching situation is possible! But what we had trouble remembering was that block scheduling was still a new concept to the parents of our new students, in particular our new first-years. Many of the structures we had put into place to inform parents in the first year of going to the block were not used in the following years, but our new parents needed that information as much as previous parents and their students had.

Just as important as helping parents to understand the new structures is providing information related to the new instructional approaches and assessment changes that parents will be seeing and hearing about. When students tell their parents they need to use the computer to, say, write a note to their friend (i.e., engage in Written

Conversation about a book), parents can often be confused and question the purpose, benefits, and challenges of such assignments if teachers have not found ways to inform them ahead of time.

ACT Testing and Review Sessions

Some schools offer ACT and SAT review sessions for juniors every fall. Spring review sessions may need to be scheduled in schools that choose the 4×4 block schedule. It may also be beneficial for counselors to identify the best testing session (fall or spring) for students based upon when they are enrolled in such classes as English and U.S. history.

Trusting the Process and Giving It Time

We don't remember the source or the person, but someone said somewhere that change takes at least three years. This was one of the best pieces of advice we had as we were meeting our challenges and learning from them. Whenever someone in the school said, "This isn't working, we need to go back to the old schedule," we kept that advice in mind and were thankful we had made a three-year commitment to making the block work. Changing instructional time affects nearly every aspect of the school, and when little remains constant, some teachers and administrators feel discomfort and others feel excitement. It's not often that educators have the opportunity to work together to create a school that is built not just on tradition but on what's best for all the learners (students, teachers, and administrators) in the building. Block scheduling offers that opportunity.

Earlier in this book, the strategy Most Important Word was described as a way to get readers to summarize a text in one word. If we were to summarize our experiences as we prepared for block scheduling in a word, that word would be *challenging*. If we were to summarize our first year of teaching on the block in a word, it would be *challenging*. We were challenged to rethink our commonly held beliefs and experiences about nearly every aspect of how we approached all of the complex and interconnected ways in which schools have traditionally operated. Block scheduling was an opportunity to create working situations that were both exciting and supportive of students and teachers. Was it easy work? In a word, no. Was it worth it? In a word, yes! Never has a challenge been more rewarding on a personal and professional level.

Appendix A: Sample Block Schedules

Copernican Plan

Period	Semester 1	Semester 2
1	English	science
2	history	math
3*	interdisciplinary seminar art PE	
4	teacher assistance psychology creative writing	

Alternate Day (aka Block 8, A/B, Odd/Even, Day 1/Day 2) with Semester-Long Classes

Period	Red Day	Gray Day
1	English	science
2	history	math
3*	art/PE	creative writing/psychology
4	Spanish	resource

4×4 Schedule

Period	Term 1	Term 2	Term 3	Term 4
1	English	English	PE	PE
2	art	mythology	science	science
3*	history	history	math	math
4	Spanish	Spanish	creative writing	psychology

(Each term is nine weeks long.)

Trimester Plan (aka 3×5 Trimester Plan)

Period	Fall	Winter	Spring
1	history	English A**	English B**
2	history	art**	art**
3*	yearbook		
4	PE	math A	math B
5	Spanish	Spanish	PE

(Each trimester is twelve weeks long. Class periods are 72 minutes long. Double class periods are 149 minutes long since no passing period is needed.)

* Lunch periods are determined by individual third-period class schedules.
** Denotes interdisciplinary class.

Appendix B: Mundelein High School Block Schedule Policies

1. Make-Up/Advancement Period

The make-up/advancement period will be scheduled each Wednesday from 1:55 P.M. to 3:45 P.M.

Any student may attend for the purpose of advancement/resource (special education).

Students with one or more absence(s) since the prior Wednesday are **required to attend in order to receive credit** for any make-up work due from the absence(s).

Any student **truant** from a class may be required, at the discretion of the teacher, to attend the make-up session. **NO** credit will be given for the make-up work. In addition, the student activities director, athletic director, or coach may require attendance for students involved in activities and experiencing academic difficulty.

Buses will run at 2:00 P.M. and again at 3:50 P.M. There will be four make-up sessions of 23 minutes each (see chart below). Consecutive sessions will total 52 minutes (23 + 23 + 6 minutes passing time).

Students may spend varying times with teachers; however, faculty will be assigned two sessions so students know when their teachers are available. For example, a first-year student might spend 52 minutes with a science teacher to make up a lab, 10 minutes with an English teacher to go over what was missed, 15 minutes with a math teacher to review for an upcoming test, and 25 minutes with a social studies teacher to make up a missed quiz. A senior with no science class might go to an elective teacher, then make up P.E. for 52 minutes, then go to an English and elective teacher. The sessions when a given department, say, English, is not offering student contact time will be devoted to departmental inservice.

The schedule charted below will rotate every term since staff members' and students' schedules will change and rotating will allow

---

These policies were put in place during the 1996–97 school year and are reviewed and revised each year.

flexibility and equity. The schedule for the first term of the 1996–97 school year will be as indicated below. Physical education is not assigned, since students can make up P.E. either during this time or at other times. P.E./Health/Dr. Ed. staff will schedule for inservice times that best fit their schedules.

Division of Time in Make-Up/Advancement Period			
Session	**Time**	**Student Contact Subject**	**Departmental Inservice**
1	1:55–2:18	science, electives	English, math, social studies
2	2:24–2:47	science, math	English, electives, social studies
3	2:53–3:16	English, math, social studies	science, electives
4	3:22–3:45	English, electives, social studies	science, math

Each department/division will schedule a one-hour meeting each month, either from 6:45 A.M. to 7:45 A.M. or from 3:30 P.M. to 4:30 P.M. Faculty meetings routinely will be held at 3:45 P.M. on Wednesdays.

The following chart indicates the rotation schedule for sessions in the make-up/advancement period through four terms.

Session Rotation for Make-Up/Advancement Period			
Term/ Session	**Time**	**Student Contact Subject**	**Departmental Inservice**
1.1	1:55–2:18	science, electives	English, math, social studies
1.2	2:24–2:47	science, math	English, electives, social studies
1.3	2:53–3:16	English, math, social studies	science, electives
1.4	3:22–3:45	English, electives, social studies	science, math
2.1	1:55–2:18	English, electives, social studies	science, math

Continued on next page

Term/ Session	Time	Student Contact Subject	Departmental Inservice
2.2	2:24–2:47	science, electives	English, math, social studies
2.3	2:53–3:16	science, math	English, electives, social studies
2.4	3:22–3:45	English, math, social studies	science, electives
3.1	1:55–2:18	English, math, social studies	science, electives
3.2	2:24–2:47	English, electives, social studies	science, math
3.3	2:53–3:16	science, electives	English, math, social studies
3.4	3:22–3:45	science, math	English, electives, social studies
4.1	1:55–2:18	science, math	English, electives, social studies
4.2	2:24–2:47	English, math, social studies	science, electives
4.3	2:53–3:16	English, electives, social studies	science, math
4.4	3:22–3:45	science, electives	English, math, social studies

2. Student Schedules

All first-years, sophomores, and juniors will be expected to have a full schedule (four classes per term). The exceptions would be juniors with a physical education waiver for the term and students with special circumstances that support an abbreviated schedule. Decisions pertaining to alternative/abbreviated schedules will include parents, dean, counselor, guidance director, and social worker. Seniors in good academic standing may take three courses per term and enter late (second period) or exit early (after third period).

Abbreviated schedules will not be considered, except in rare cases, until the student reaches age sixteen (dropout age). Students electing periods 0, 5, 6, and 7 (should an extended day become an option) will not be allowed to change schedules, as this would affect staffing. Again, exceptions may be necessary as circumstances change.

Students who fail a class may have to wait a term before reentering/repeating a class. Some "light" sections may be scheduled to accommodate returning students who failed previously. Students who fail half of their classes due to truancy will be reviewed and **may** be placed in an alternative setting for the remainder of the term if such an appropriate setting is available.

The Session Rotation for Make-Up/Advancement Period grid (see above) reflects possible schedules for the 1996–97 school year. An attempt will be made to reflect the daily schedule on the school calendar and in the student handbook so that everyone knows what the schedule is for the day.

3. Extracurricular Activities

Extracurriculars will continue to be conducted outside of the school day. Students taking part in activities may be accommodated on Wednesdays from 1:55 to 3:45 P.M. so they do not have to leave the building and return, as this might create a transportation problem. Students participating in activities and students experiencing academic difficulty may be **required** to attend the Wednesday make-up.

Possible exceptions to the practices described above include occasional Inter-Class Council meetings during lunch periods and athletic teams and coaches leaving early on Wednesdays when it benefits scheduling.

The other issue is one of student schedules and absences due to extracurricular participation. A student who is absent due to a school sponsored **curricular** or **extracurricular** activity will be expected to attend the Wednesday make-up session for the classes missed. However, we are going to have to be sensitive to the fact that the student has no control over the absence(s). The best (worst) example would be a golf member who must miss three full days for conference, regional, and sectional meets **plus** early dismissals for other meets. This golfer could possibly miss fourth-period class as many as six or seven times during the first term. This would definitely impact other decisions if there are other absences. It is possible then that a golfer might not be approved for another absence during that term (say, for a college visit) or be excused for a match if there have been numerous days of absence due to illness.

4. Homework

The concern teachers have for students who come to class without home-work completed is fairly typical in most schools. It's often difficult to proceed with the next lesson if many students have not done the pre-paratory work. When small numbers of students don't do their home-work, the teacher can go on with the lesson as planned, but participa-tion and success in subsequent activities is usually limited to students who completed their homework prior to class. One class period on the block schedule is often looked at as two class periods, and from such a perspective the concern for homework becomes greater. If a student doesn't do the homework, the next "two days" of class will suffer.

Schoolwide Committee Decision

Homework will remain an integral part of the learning experience. The expectation is that students will come to class prepared and with home-work completed. Each department will develop a philosophy indicat-ing the role of homework in the learning process and in the determina-tion of the semester grade. The department will address the following issues when developing the homework policy.

1. Homework will be an expectation.
2. Homework will be defined as preparation outside of the class-room that is meaningful and relevant to the curriculum and learning experience.
3. Time should not be provided for students to do homework during the class period. The class period should be dedicated to instructional activities. Guided practice is appropriate as a vehicle for assisting student learning and in preparation for doing the homework assignment.
4. The department as a whole, and faculty members as individu-als, need to be sensitive to the change in the daily pattern of the student's schedule. Students will not have study time in their schedules except for the Wednesday make-up/advance-ment session.
5. Homework should be used in determining the participation grade that is calculated in determining the semester grade.
6. Block scheduling (ninety-minute classes) does not necessarily mean doubling homework assignments.
7. If a problem exists with attendance, preparation, or homework, the parent and/or counselor should be notified with the inten-tion of getting support in addressing the issue.
8. At the discretion of the teacher, students may be required to

attend the Wednesday make-up session to work with the teacher on their homework.

9. It is the students' responsibility to secure make-up assignments on the day of their return after an absence. The student is allowed two days for each day absent to complete the work. Attendance at the Wednesday make-up session is required in order to receive credit for work completed.

English Department Homework Decision

The English department has developed a philosophy indicating the role of homework in the learning process and in the determination of the semester grade. We believe that homework is an essential component of the learning process. Further, we believe that

- individual teachers should develop their own criteria for assigning credit to and for homework,
- homework assignments should call on students to use all the community tools and resources not available to students in school or during school hours,
- homework should be an extension of the types of learning experiences occurring in the classroom,
- homework should have as its focus activities that the individual student needs to accomplish in order to participate in the following class period, and
- homework experiences should resemble those with which the student is already familiar from class, including but not limited to:
    - researching topics and gathering materials at local libraries,
    - reading, rereading, and reviewing material for the next lesson,
    - preparing for small-group discussion,
    - drafting essays, poetry, and fiction,
    - typing class assignments,
    - proofreading and editing written work,
    - pursuing adjunct materials and topics,
    - meeting with classmates for group projects,
    - viewing commercial and educational videotapes,
    - scheduling and conducting interviews and surveys,
    - reading free-choice novels,
    - reading Core and Enrichment literature,
    - reflecting on previous work and group activity,

- organizing portfolios, and
- creating curriculum-related artwork.

5. Open House and Parent/Teacher Conferences

Open House will be held early in the school year. At this time, students will be scheduled into only four classes and, potentially, only one-fourth of their yearly schedule. Therefore, we will look at a different format. We are considering departmental presentations with the opportunity for parents to meet, in an informal setting, the faculty with whom their students are or will be studying during the school year. A special session for parents of first-year students will continue to precede the main program.

Parent/teacher Conferences will be scheduled for the midpoint of the first term and of the third term. The total length of the conferences should be reduced due to the fact that faculty will have approximately half their present student load. During the second and fourth terms, time will be set aside during the department inservice session on selected Wednesdays for conferences in person or by phone.

We will **not** have early dismissals to accommodate Open House or parent/teacher conferences. Therefore, these events will not intrude upon or reduce instructional time as they have in the past. Faculty will receive compensation time by leaving at 2:00 P.M. on the Wednesday preceding Thanksgiving, scheduling full inservice days from 7:45 A.M. to 1:45 P.M., and/or other approaches as agreed upon by the principal and the faculty member.

6. Flex Schedule/Compensation Time

Deans, counselors, and teaching faculty may choose flex schedules for a term, for a year, or for individual/department reasons.

Flex schedules may include periods 0, 5, 6, or 7. There may be combinations as well. For example, a teacher could teach 0, 1, 2 and have 3/lunch as preparation or teach 2, 3, 4 and have 5 as preparation. Also, a teacher could teach 3, 4, and the first half of 5 and then do preparation for the second half of 5 and teach a class on Tuesday and Thursday from 5:20 P.M. to 8:50 P.M. or 4:00 P.M. to 7:30 P.M. Classes could also meet for two hours and twenty-five minutes for three evenings.

All flex schedules will depend upon student demand, matching teacher volunteers for the classes students want, and monitoring/supervising (availability of security personnel). The demand may also require a review of staffing with deans, administrators, a nurse, technology personnel, media center personnel, etc. We also need to monitor student and staff accessibility to each other, as lines of communication must be kept open. **If a flex schedule of any kind is of interest to you, please notify the principal's office.**

Compensation time will be looked at as a way of meeting special needs and not as a common practice for faculty when they are meeting the requirements of their job. When looking at compensation time, we need to consider availability of staff to parents, other staff, and students, as well as office coverage (deans, counselors, etc.). Compensation time should not be viewed as an hour-for-hour trade. For example, counselors may choose (on a rotating basis so the office is covered) to work from noon to 8:00 P.M. during registration. However, attendance at the Class of 2000 Night or College Night should be viewed as a regular part of faculty responsibility and is not eligible for compensation time. However, we are allowing faculty compensation time for such things as Open House and parent/teacher conferences that requires all faculty to be in attendance outside the school day.

Flex time and compensation time will have to be reviewed as we proceed during the 1996–97 school year.

7. Teacher Evaluation

Tenured teachers shall be involved in the formal evaluation process at least once every two years. The formal evaluation process consists of peer observation by another tenured teacher, meetings between the two teachers for the purposes of processing information on the lesson and providing feedback, a written self-evaluation on the part of the teacher being evaluated, and a closing conference between the teacher and an administrator selected from the list of qualified administrators. By October 1, the teacher being evaluated shall select his or her peer collaborator and evaluator by completing the Evaluation Observation form and filing it in the superintendent's office. The formal evaluation must be completed by April 30, with the completed form again filed in the superintendent's office.

A committee will be formed at the beginning of the 1996–97 school year to assess this process and collect data on peer observations in order to make recommendations for improvement in the evaluation process. After a two-year period (during which all tenured teachers will have completed this cycle)—that is, at the end of the 1997–98 school year—the committee will make recommendations for change.

The policies and procedures for nontenured teachers will remain in their present form.

8. Deans' and Counselors' Access to Students

Everyone understands the need for deans, counselors, social workers, psychologists, and other special support services staff to have access to students during the school day. The desire is to make this access as unintrusive to the classroom environment as possible. These persons will make themselves available before school, after school, and during lunch periods.

However, the need for access to students during class time is a reality. Efforts will be made to minimize disruption and spread the requests throughout the day. Faculty will have discretion as to when during the period the student is sent unless the pass says "now" or indicates a time for a group session. When making that decision, plan on the student being gone twenty minutes.

Teachers may request that a specific student **not be removed** from that class if the student's attendance and/or academic performance is problematic. Every attempt will be made to accommodate such requests.

9. First-Year MESH Orientation

First-Year Orientation will take place on the same day as the teacher institute. The following day of orientation will be for all students, not just incoming first-year students. The only faculty involvement will be faculty who have first-year classes or first-year advisory. **Faculty will be involved only during the mini schedule from 11:50 A.M. to 1:00 P.M., when students will attend their Term 1 first-, second-, third-, and fourth-period classes.**

Schedule

8:00 A.M.–11:00 A.M.	MESH (junior/senior leaders only)
11:00 A.M.–11:45 A.M.	Lunch
11:50 A.M.–1:00 P.M.	Mini schedule

1. 11:50 A.M.–12:00
2. 12:05 P.M.–12:15 P.M.
(Advisory: 12:20 P.M.–12:30 P.M.)
3. 12:35 P.M.–12:45 P.M.
4. 12:50 P.M.–1:00 P.M.

1:05 P.M.–1:25 P.M.	Assembly
1:30 P.M.	First-year exit

10. First-Year Advisory

Staff (faculty, instructional aides, classified) will be matched, on a voluntary basis, with five to seven first-year students each. There will be an agenda of topics (study skills, how to dress for homecoming, expected behavior at the NHS assembly, etc.), as well as the expectation that the advisor will support the student and monitor/coordinate with faculty, counselors, deans, and parents. Staff will be given a preference as to when their advisory meeting(s) will be scheduled, and, if possible, all students assigned will be assigned to the same counselor.

All advisory meetings will be scheduled (considering the staff member's preference) **either** from 7:40 A.M. to 7:55 A.M. or during the beginning of a lunch period **once** per week. We will avoid Wednesdays. Staff may volunteer for one advisory group or two advisory groups. Advisory group sizes will depend on the number of staff volunteers. For example, 70 total volunteers for 350 first-year students would mean 5 first-years per group; 50 total volunteers would mean 7 first-years per group.

The assignment will be considered to be a minimum of thirty minutes per week (fifteen-minute meeting and fifteen minutes of follow-up, contact with staff/parents, etc.). The staff will be allowed thirty minutes of compensation time each week for each advisory group to which the staff member is assigned. This arrangement will be by mutual agreement between the staff member and the principal. For example, a staff member volunteering for one first-year advisory group may choose to leave each Friday at 3:15 P.M. rather than 3:45 P.M.

11. Graduation Requirements

Requirements for the class of 2000 will be as follows:

English	4.0 credits
Mathematics	2.0 credits
Introduction to Science	0.5 credit
Science	2.0 credits
*Global Studies or World History	1.0 credit
U.S. History	1.0 credit
Consumer Economics or equivalent	0.5 credit
Social Studies electives	0.5 credit
Health Education	0.5 credit

Keyboarding & Applications	0.5 credit
Safety Education	0.5 credit
Physical Education/waiver	3.5 credits
**Electives	11.5 credits
TOTAL	28.0 CREDITS

*Beginning with the class of 2000, students will be required to pass World History or Global Studies (or a transfer equivalent) as a prerequisite for U.S. History.

**A total of three elective credits need to be earned in three of these elective areas: foreign language, art, journalism, industrial education, consumer and family sciences, business education, music, language arts lab, theatre, and speech.

The total number of elective credits for transfer students will be based on credit-earning potential by graduation but must include three elective area requirements.

Graduation requirements for transfer students will be determined by their potential for earning credits, less four credits.

Requirements for the class of 1999 will be 26.5 credits. Requirements for the class of 1998 will be 24.5 credits, and the requirements for the class of 1997 will be 22.5 credits.

Credit equivalent needed for class status/privileges:

sophomore	7 credits
junior	14 credits
senior	21 credits

12. Field Trips

Even among teachers who see the educational value of field trips, there is usually concern for the amount of class time students miss if they are involved in a field trip. This concern increases when plans are being made for block scheduling. Again, one day out of school for a field trip on the block schedule is like missing two days of class on a traditional schedule.

Schoolwide Committee Decision

Field trips during the school day will be discouraged. Field trips outside of the school day will be encouraged. If the field trip is curricular and related to the classroom, the faculty member(s) will be compensated at a rate equivalent to what a substitute would have been paid if the field trip had taken place during the school day. A field trip scheduled during the school day will be disruptive to other learning environments the student will miss on that given day. We all need to be sensitive to the importance of students being in the classroom. We also need to recognize the value and importance of curricularly related authentic experiences outside of the classroom. All faculty/departments should reexamine the role and value of field trips in their curriculums. The following will all be taken into consideration and used as guidelines when determining the approval of a field trip during the school day and in deciding whether a given individual student will be allowed to attend.

Department

1. Is the field trip curriculum-related?
2. Can the field trip take place outside the school day?
3. NO field trips during the first or last week of a term.

Teacher

4. The request must be submitted and distributed two weeks prior to the trip. Any faculty member may communicate a concern about a specific student's attendance on a field trip.
5. No field trips should be scheduled on a Wednesday (make-up day). Any student missing classes due to a field trip must attend the Wednesday make-up session in order to earn credit for make-up work.
6. Field trips completed within the ninety-minute block of a given class will be encouraged as students will be considered present and will not miss other classes.

Student

7. Field trips will be considered a privilege. Therefore, any student with an unexcused absence in any class within fifteen school days of the field trip will not be allowed to attend. A student with two unexcused absences will not be permitted to attend a field trip for the remainder of the term.
8. The student's attendance record will be taken into consideration, as field trips are counted like any other absence. The excessive absence policy will be taken into consideration.
9. Students will have to make decisions about participating in field trips during the school day. Each student will be limited to two field trips that take place during the school day or cause absences from other classes.
10. Exceptions will have to be made.

Discussion of English Department's Decisions Related to Field Trips

We generated a list of the field trips we offered (both outside-of-school field trips and those that were inhouse) for each of the courses we taught. We discovered that certain courses, such as Senior Project (where students study a topic of interest with a mentor), were dependent on field trips. Others, such as Expressions: Literature and the Arts, were greatly enhanced by field trips to the art museum, plays, and concerts. It was decided that these courses could be scheduled during first or last period, which would allow students in Senior Project to begin their school day earlier than the 8:00 bell or extend their day beyond 3:15. The Expressions class could leave for a field trip as early as 1:45 if it were scheduled as a fourth-period class, and they could return as late as evening. Other classes that took short trips were scheduled as much as possible during the period that included lunch, which in our case was third period. This way, teachers had a little over two hours (including passing times) in which to take their students out of the building.

We discovered that larger blocks of time gave us the opportunity to use more of the community resources that are available for class-period field trips. On the block schedule, one English teacher took her students to an elementary school to teach a lesson related to their research, and a creative writing teacher took her students to a poetry reading by Luis Rodriguez at a nearby community college. The use of guest speakers on the traditional schedule was difficult, but on the block schedule we could set up many more "inhouse" field trips for several classes, which reduced the need for full-day trips outside of the building. For example, the teacher of autistic students and her class spoke to first-year English classes, a Native American artist and writer conducted workshops for English and art students, and featured speakers for inhouse field trips included sportswriter Rick Telander and authors Lois Duncan and Chris Crutcher.

13. Assemblies

Assemblies will be kept at a minimum. An attempt will be made to spread assemblies out over the four terms. For example:

Term	Assembly
1	Opening of school
2	Homecoming National Honor Society induction
3	Turnabout dance

4	Honors Day
	Students Against Destructive Decisions (SADD)

All other assembly-type activities will be run through the lunch periods. This would include things like Pathfinder meetings, Jr./Sr. meetings (meetings with counselors), class officer speeches, teen issues, prom fashion show, etc. An effort will be made to have the assemblies at various times of the day depending upon the nature of the assembly.

<u>**All assemblies will be held in the gymnasium in 1996–97. Plan accordingly.**</u> Rare exceptions may be accommodated as the opportunity arises and if deemed appropriate.

14. Add/Drops and Suspensions

A student must register within the first five days of a term to be eligible to earn credit. There will be three <u>**centers**</u> to serve students while not in a regular class. These centers <u>**may**</u> overlap in some cases in order to better meet student needs.

<u>**Transfer Center:**</u> Transfer students will be accommodated until they are in a position to enter regular classes at the beginning of a term. They will enter either ahead or behind our curriculum and may earn some credit(s) as determined by their transfer records.

<u>**Advancement Center:**</u> Staffed by faculty from selected curricular areas, the Advancement Center will serve as a support system for English, math, special education, the gifted program, etc. Students from regular classrooms may be sent for support/enhancement within departmental guidelines and with approval. Also, students who "outgrow" our curriculum will have access (through computer programs) to advanced study.

<u>**Alternative Center:**</u> Students who have been dropped from a class (i.e., for being truant from class [TFC]), have poor attendance, multiple failures, etc., <u>**may**</u> be placed in the Alternative Center for a period or for part of their day. Placement will be determined by the dean, counselor, parent, and director of guidance. The program will be primarily computer-driven, and each department will be involved in determining <u>**how much, if any,**</u> credit is given. A student dropped from a class may also be dropped from other classes to accommodate this placement. Some cases may also require an abbreviated schedule for the remainder of the term.

We will ease into these programs during the 1996–97 school year. Building and room limitations as well as program development will determine how quickly we move ahead.

In-school suspension will be reinstated as one of the options available to the dean's office. Students are expected to use this time to do school work that they would be missing. Out-of-school suspension will continue to be used; however, alternatives will be explored with parental approval.

Any student suspended from school for a Class 1 offense **may** be recommended for expulsion for the remainder of the term due to the number of days the student will miss classes. Any student suspended from school for a second Class 1 offense during the same term **will** be recommended for expulsion for a **minimum** of the remainder of the term. The seriousness of a Class 1 offense will continue to determine whether a recommendation for expulsion will be initiated.

In all of the situations pertaining to drops, adds, suspensions, transfer students, etc., the individual circumstance will determine the recommendation.

15. Grading

We need to begin with a statement of philosophy. Grades should be determined by a minimum standard required for continuing success in the curriculum. **In addition,** student growth, effort, participation, attendance, and contribution to the learning of others must also be taken into consideration. The expectation for each student may differ even if the minimum standard is established. The expectation is that every student should grow and improve as he or she goes through the experience of the curriculum.

Each department will develop a grading philosophy and policy. This will be presented to the Curriculum Committee for approval. The Curriculum Committee will determine whether the department's grading policy is consistent with the curriculum, assessment procedures, and other grading policies.

The term's work will constitute 80 percent of the term grade, and the final assessment will constitute 20 percent of the term grade. All curricula will have an identified final assessment and a guide explaining how the 80 percent of the grade is determined for the work completed during the term.

What are students graded on and how much does it count? That 80 percent should include minimum standard, growth, effort, attendance/participation, and contributions.

At the beginning of each course, students will receive written information regarding course requirements, testing, and averaging of grades. Letter grades and their descriptions are as follows:

A (100–90)	Excellent
B (89–80)	Above Average
C (79–70)	Average
D (69–60)	Below Average/Danger of Failing
F (59–0)	Failing Grade (No Credit)

The most important factor in the determination of a grade is the mastery of the subject matter. Other factors which teachers will consider are: attitude, effort, class participation, homework, test performance, and the development of skills. It is the responsibility of each student to thoroughly understand the procedures of how his or her grades are attained. It is the responsibility of the teacher to clarify procedures **in written form** at the beginning of the semester.

Teachers will have discretion in reporting the semester grade. However, the grade must be consistent with the departmental philosophy and with policy, as well as defendable to the student and parent.

The E grade will be eliminated. Pluses and minuses will be used for progress grades but not for semester grades. No specific distinctive system will be used to determine the semester grade.

16. Title I

In many schools students who are having difficulty with reading receive support services from a Title I program. The work students are doing in their Title I class usually complements or is coordinated with their English class. When moving to the block schedule, simply transferring the way of doing Title I as a separate class period on the traditional schedule to a full ninety-minute class on the block schedule may not be the best way to provide the reading support that these students need. The English teachers at MHS reasoned that students in these classes are not particularly enamored with the subject to begin with, so three hours of English and English-related courses in one day was probably not the best plan for students or their teachers. Reconceptualizing the way support is provided for these students is something that schools moving to the block schedule should consider.

Schoolwide Committee Decision

Title I will support English and math by providing support in the Advancement Center as well as in the classroom. English and math staff will determine the best utilization of their staff. To begin with, English and math staff will be assigned, on a rotating basis, to staff the Advancement Center. Specifics will be determined by staffing needs and patterns for each department. Part of this assignment may involve working with transfer students, working with teachers in assisting with the delivery of the curriculum, and spending time in the classroom to team-teach. The center will not be considered a make-up area.

For example, an English teacher (or aide) could be assigned to the Advancement Center for half of a period each day (forty-five minutes) and to a first-year English class for half of a period each day (forty-five minutes). This would provide the general support/opportunity in the Advancement Center and the basic support for English students. In math, a similar concept could be used to support all math students and allow for more individualized attention.

This need is created by the elimination of Language Arts Lab [the Mundelein class name for Title I] and general math. A support system, as described above, needs to be in place.

English Department Plan for the Advancement Center

The MHS English Department's plan for the Advancement Center could best be described as a combination of a writing center and the one-on-one work that special education teachers in many schools do with students identified for their caseload. Rather than being a drop-in area for students to receive help just with their writing, the center will be a place where individual students and groups can work with an English or reading teacher on reading, writing, discussion, research, and small-group or individual presentations. In addition, teachers working in the Advancement Center for one class period will be assigned a caseload of students who have met the Title I criteria. Regularly scheduled meetings between caseload students and their Advancement Center teacher will be arranged with the Title I students' English teachers. (The Advancement Center is described in detail in Chapter 7.)

17. Attendance Requirements

<u>**Regular attendance is necessary for success in school.**</u> A record of punctuality and attendance is maintained for each student. Regular attendance is required for all students. For students under age sixteen, attendance is required by state law. If the law is violated, the student and the parents are subject to legal action. Students and parents are going to have to closely monitor attendance in each individual class. **<u>An absence is an absence,</u>** whether excused, unexcused, due to a field trip, or another cause. Absences from class will affect learning and may affect a student's performance and grade. When a student has reached

five absences in a term (forty-four days) the student is considered to be excessively absent. After the fifth absence occurs, the school will expect communication with the parent and documentation explaining the need for the student's absences. The inability to provide satisfactory explanation/documentation will result in consequences that will adversely affect the student's grade, as no credit will be given for missed work or tests after the fifth absence. **Without** extra effort on the part of the student, the possibility of passing the course diminishes after each absence beyond five. **Participation is used in determining grades, and a student cannot participate unless the student is in class.**

Absence Procedures

In cases of absence, the parent or guardian must call the school on the day of the absence. We have installed an answering machine, and a message may be left before or after school hours. Make sure the student's name, date, and reason for absence, as well as the name of the person making the call, are given in the message.

The following numbers should be called at the times given:

4:30 A.M.–6:30 A.M.	949-2200, press 4 (answering machine)
6:30 A.M.–7:45 A.M.	949-2200 (receptionist)
7:45 A.M.–3:30 P.M.	949-2200, extension 243 (attendance office)

It is the **student's responsibility** to make sure a call is received by 3:30 P.M. the day of the absence. Failure to report an absence on the day of the absence **may result in discipline being assigned and/or no academic credit being given for the school day.**

In keeping with Section 26-2A of the Illinois State Code, Mundelein High School considers the following circumstances to be valid causes for a student's absence:

1. Illness
2. Religious holidays
3. Death in the family
4. Valid doctor or court appointment (A student must present valid documentation upon his or her return to school.)
5. Family emergency (Family emergencies need to be cleared by a dean if they are to be excused.)

Make-Up for Excused Absences

It is the student's responsibility to secure the make-up work when he or she is excusably absent. This should be done the day he or she returns.

For each day a student is absent, he or she will be allowed two days to make up the work. Therefore, if a student is out for two days and is excusably absent, the student will have four days to make up the work. **The student must attend the Wednesday make-up period (2:00 P.M.– 3:45 P.M.) immediately following the absence in order to receive credit for make-up work.**

Excessive Absences

A student who is excessively absent from school on a whole- or part-day basis may be required to provide a doctor's note. Excessive absence is defined as **five** days absent during a nine-week term. In no way should this policy suggest that a student is entitled to a certain number of absences. A student exhibiting an absence pattern will be subject to disciplinary action. This will not apply when hospitalization or special out-of-school care is necessary. **Homebound instruction should be requested when consecutive absences beyond five days are antici-pated.** Parents are required to contact the Homebound Coordinator to request the forms that need to be completed by a doctor licensed to prac-tice medicine in the State of Illinois. Instruction is provided by certified visiting teachers at no cost to the parents or guardians. Students who are unable to provide a doctor's excuse may receive a failing grade for each day of class missed during the nine-week term.

Tardies

Tardies are excused for emergency reasons only. Oversleeping, automo-bile problems, missing the bus, etc., are not considered emergencies. Parents are required to call the attendance office (949-2200, extension 243) to explain the reason for the tardy. Unexcused tardiness is defined as an unauthorized late arrival to class. **Four unexcused tardies in a class shall constitute one truancy from class.**

Truancy

Truancy from class shall be handled according to the following proce-dure.

First Unexcused Absence
1. The classroom teacher informs the student of the truancy sta-tus.
2. The dean's office will call the parent and generate a letter to the parent.
3. The unexcused absence will result in no credit being given for all work missed.

4. **The student will lose privileges for fifteen school days.**

Second Unexcused Absence

1. The dean's office will generate a referral informing the teacher, parent, and counselor of the unexcused absence.

2. **The counselor/dean holds a conference with the student and calls the parents to inform them and explain the consequence of a third truancy from class.**

3. The unexcused absence will result in no credit being given for all work missed.

4. **The student will lose privileges for thirty school days.**

Third Unexcused Absence

1. The dean will inform the teacher, student, and parent that a failing grade will be issued for the class.

2. **The student will lose privileges for the remainder of the term and the entire next term (forty-four days).**

3. **The student may be allowed to remain in the class for the remainder of the term. If the teacher, dean, and counselor determine that the student is to be removed for the remainder of the term, the student will be placed in a disciplinary hall.**

Any student who has been removed from 50 percent of his or her classes may be referred to the District Hearing Officer for a multidisciplinary education assessment. **Failure due to TFCs and/or removal in 50 percent or more of his or her classes may result in a recommendation for expulsion for the remainder of the term.** All tests or assignments on the day of the truancy will receive a failing grade. Students who are truant the day before a test or assignment may be required to take the test or turn in the assignment on the day they return.

Truancy Make-Up

Any student truant from a class may be required to make up all work for no credit to insure that the student remains current with the other students. **At the teacher's discretion, attendance at the Wednesday (2:00 P.M.–3:45 P.M.) make-up period is required. Failure to attend will result in additional loss of privileges.**

Truant from School

Students truant from half or more than half of their scheduled classes during one school day will be considered truant from school. Students truant from school will receive one day of Saturday School for each half day of school missed.

Lengthy/Advanced Absences

Whenever possible, assignments should be collected for a student when an absence of two days or longer is expected. Call 949-2200 to arrange for student assignments. **Assignments may be picked up at 3:30 P.M. on the day following the request. When absences of over a week are anticipated, parents should talk to the counseling department about homebound instruction.**

Occasionally, students may be aware of expected dates of absence. Before these anticipated absences, the student is to pick up and complete an advanced absence request form from the dean's office. For clarification, contact the dean's office. **Family vacations during school terms should be avoided as academic failure may occur.**

Attendance Requirements for Participating in School-Sponsored Activities

A student must attend class or be participating in school-sponsored activities during the school day if he or she wishes to participate in any school-sponsored (i.e., athletic, theatre, band, etc.) activity on that day. No student shall be permitted to participate in any activity including practice sessions if he or she was absent from school and returns to school after the end of the school day in an attempt to be present only for the school-sponsored activity. Students absent in the morning must arrive at school by 11:15 A.M. in order to practice or compete in athletic activities on that day. Students leaving school for the day before 11:15 A.M. also may not participate or compete that day.

Whenever a student has been absent from school on a Friday prior to a Saturday-scheduled activity, he or she will be eligible to participate at the discretion of the coach or faculty sponsor of the activity.

Procedure for Leaving School or School Grounds

1. The attendance office must have a call from the student's parent/guardian, and the dean must approve the reason for leaving before a student will be allowed to leave campus.

2. Once the call has been received and the reason for leaving has been approved, the student must sign out at the attendance office. If the student returns before the end of his or her school day, he or she must sign in at the attendance office.

Any student leaving the building or campus once he or she has arrived at school without following these procedures will be considered truant.

18. Progress Reports/Semester Grades

Progress reports will be sent at the midpoint (four weeks) of each term. These will be computer generated, and each student will receive a report for each class. The progress report will include a **grade in progress** (e.g., C+ or A-), as well as comments that explain and support the grade in progress. The report will include general comments as well as comments specifically designed for each department. The intent of creating this boilerplate text is to provide teachers with comments which will explain the grades recorded. **In addition,** handwritten progress reports may be generated anytime during the term to indicate changes in performance and/or danger of failing. These reports will be sent every Tuesday and Friday through a central collection area.

    Report cards will use the same format as progress reports. The only grade reported will be the final grade for the term. Once again, comments will be available to explain/support the final grade.

    A special provision will need to be in place for classes that meet every other day for eighty-eight days for a 0.5 credit.

    Each department will generate its specific comments, and a faculty committee will be formed to develop the general comments.

19. Final Exams

There will be no special final exam schedule. **NO** student exemption from final exams will be permitted. All final exams/assessments are to be part of the learning experience and consistent with curricular, instructional, and assessment procedures during the term. Each department will determine the format for final exams. The value to be placed on the final exam/assessment will be 20 percent of the term grade.

    Exam dates will be coordinated by the directors of instruction to insure that students have adequate study and preparation time.

20. Physical Education/AVC (Area Vocational Center) Waivers

Junior and senior athletes will have to apply for waivers by March 15, 1996, for the 1996–97 school year. Waivers will be approved by the **term,** not the season. A junior or senior participating in one sport may waive one physical education class; those participating in two sports may waive two physical education classes. An athlete participating in a winter sport which covers two terms must enroll in physical education during either term 1 or term 4. Each physical education waiver will reduce the graduation requirement for the student athlete by 0.5 credit. Students waived from physical education for a term may elect to take another course. When waived, the student may enter late, exit early, or extend his or her lunch period during the waiver. Any student who quits a sport will be treated as if the waiver was not granted and must make up the physical education credit.

AVC will be available during first session (8:20 A.M.–10:20 A.M.). Students will return to Mundelein High School in time to eat lunch and attend third- and fourth-period classes. For the most part, AVC students requiring a waiver from physical education will be those enrolled in cosmetology.

21. Announcements

Announcements over the PA system will be made at the beginning of fourth period on Monday, during the third period(s) on Tuesday, during the beginning of second period on Thursday, and at the end of first period on Friday (no announcements will be made on Wednesdays). No announcements that are included in or should be included in the written announcements will be read over the PA system.

22. Failures

Every attempt should be made to assist every student in his or her efforts to be successful. However, we will have students who will fail due to TFCs, disruptive behavior leading to out-of-school suspension (OSS), nondiligence, and general failures.

1. A student who TFC's out of one class will receive a failing grade for the term and will stay in class (if that is the decision of the teacher, counselor, and dean), or be removed from class and be assigned an abbreviated schedule, or be placed in a disciplinary study period.

   A student who TFC's out of two or more classes will be required to attend a meeting with his or her teachers, parents, counselor, dean, and social worker and/or school psychologist, if appropriate, to determine what to do to help the student succeed. In addition to the possibilities above, the student may be considered for an alternative placement or may be recommended for **expulsion** for the remainder of the term.

2. Any student's behavior leading to two out-of-school suspensions due to Class 1 offenses during a term will be recommended for **expulsion** for the remainder of the term. This is

due to the combination of disruptive behavior and number of days missed in a forty-four-day term.

3. Failures due to nondiligence may lead to adjustments in class assignments, abbreviated schedules, or alternate placement.

4. General-failure students will not be able to repeat a class until the next time it is offered. Students may be able to continue in one-credit courses, after failing the first term, if the department feels that it is appropriate. For example, a student failing algebra or Spanish I may not be allowed to continue with the second term of the course. However, a student in World History, English, or science would be allowed to enter the second term after failing the first term. Placement in courses following a failure will **not** be automatically accommodated and will be made to build slightly smaller sections during terms 2, 3, and 4 to accommodate reentering students who previously failed without overloading classes.

Each department will need to develop a philosophy and procedures designed to lower the failure rate and to accommodate failures within their own department.

23. Student Privileges

Student privileges are granted to students who have attained the required number of credits for class status and are responsible community members. Any school infraction may lead to removal of some or all privileges. In addition, all students with excellent **attendance records** and/or excellent **academic records** and/or excellent **citizenship records** will be eligible for a variety of rewards.

1. Seniors may:

   a. park a vehicle in the school parking lot if it is properly registered and properly stickered.

   b. leave school during their regularly scheduled lunch period.

   c. enter the building late or leave early if their schedule does not require them to be there all day, and they may have access to the building as long as they produce their ID card upon request.

2. Juniors may:

   a. park a vehicle in the school parking lot if it is properly registered and properly stickered. (May be limited by availability of parking spaces).

   b. leave school during their regularly scheduled lunch period.

3. Sophomores may:

   a. remain in the lunchroom, go to the Media Center, or use the courtyard (when classes are not in session) during the second twenty-five minutes of their lunch period.

   b. sit anywhere in the cafeteria during their lunch period.

   c. attend optional assemblies that are offered during the school day.

4. First-year students may:

   a. remain in the lunchroom or go to the Media Center during the second twenty-five minutes of their lunch period.

   b. sit anywhere in the cafeteria during their lunch period.

   c. attend optional assemblies that are offered during the school day.

Examples of possible rewards to be made available to eligible students each term:

1. Free lunch hosted by deans (pizza, hamburgers, hot dogs)
2. Theatre tickets
3. Dance tickets
   a. Holiday
   b. Valentine's
   c. Prom
4. Variety Show tickets
5. Breakfast/lunch tickets
6. Car wash tickets
7. Select parking spots
8. Prime registration for Driver Education
9. Special table in cafeteria
10. Early registration—select class and teacher
11. Prime seating—plays, concerts, Variety Show, basketball
12. Sophomore—if you have perfect attendance and no discipline for one term, you get to go out for lunch one day a week
13. Periodic drawings (CDs, tapes, fast-food meal certificates)
14. Use of discount cards
15. Canteen coupons
16. Cookie coupons
17. Recognition (picture and name in glass case)
18. Certificates/letters from deans

24. Student Support

Two programs will be in place to support students as we move to the block schedule: the Advancement Center and NovaNET.

Advancement Center

The Advancement Center will serve all students and curriculums in a variety of ways. The concept of the Advancement Center was presented by the English department in the form of a curriculum proposal and was recommended by the Curriculum Committee, supported by the administration, and adopted by the Board of Education. The Advancement Center will be staffed by English teachers (as in the curriculum presented) to support the English curriculum and students. This is due primarily to the fact that the English lab curriculum has been eliminated. The Advancement Center will also include a math teacher for half the period. The math teacher will be in the pre-algebra classroom the other half of the period (Title I grant). The English teacher and math teacher will be available to assist students in other curricular areas and to assist **transfer students** as they make their transition to Mundelein High School and adjust to block-schedule curriculum.

NovaNET

NovaNET is a computerized learning program (see http://www.ncslearn.com/novanet/). The NovaNET program will serve our at-risk students as well as students who outgrow our curriculum. This may be used as a temporary placement for an at-risk student until he or she can begin a new term. It may also be used for students as an intervention prior to other more formal steps. Support for the reasons for the placement will be addressed through support services.

NovaNET will also be capable of servicing the few students we have who outgrow our curricular areas. The system can provide courses at the high school and college levels. Credit will be generated by the NovaNET program. Departments will be involved in establishing criteria/expectations for issuing credit.

The NovaNET area will be staffed with certified staff and with aide(s) as numbers grow.

Appendix C: Time Management Samples— Traditional Schedule versus Block Schedule

A Literature Lesson

Planning for two days on the traditional schedule as if it were one day on the block schedule:

Monday		**Tuesday**	
5 min.	Attendance Return papers Announcements	5 min.	Attendance Return papers Announcements
20 min.	Read *Black Boy*	20 min.	Literature discussion
10 min.	Journal writing	20 min.	Large group share
10 min.	Share questions/ideas to take to discussion on Tuesday	5 min.	Written reflections on content and process
5 min.	Written reflections on content and process		

The same lesson on the block schedule might look like this:

5 min.	Attendance Return papers Announcements
20 min.	Read *Black Boy*
10 min.	Journal writing
25 min.	Literature discussion
20 min.	Large group share
10 min.	Written reflections on content and process

A Writing Lesson

Wednesday		Thursday	
5 min.	Attendance Return papers Announcements	5 min.	Attendance Return papers Announcements
20 min.	Revise rough drafts	30 min.	Authors' circles
25 min.	Computer lab	15 min.	Revise drafts

The same lesson on the block schedule might look like this:

5 min.	Attendance Return papers Announcements
15 min.	Revise rough drafts
30 min.	Computer lab
30 min.	Authors' circles
10 min.	Revise drafts

Appendix D: Strategy Descriptions

Authors' Circle

In this strategy, students read their piece of writing aloud to the other authors in the circle, which could mean the whole class or a group of three to four students (Harste, Short, and Burke 1988). Listeners respond aloud by discussing what they hear in the writing, with special attention to what they find effective. They can also comment on the meaning of the piece and raise questions about parts where they feel the text is unclear or needs more information. Listeners need to remember that good questions and specific comments will help the writer with revisions. The writer may revise and return a piece to Authors' Circle several times before entering the editing and publishing stages.

Benefits of Authors' Circle include the following:

1. Authors' Circle demonstrates to students that their first concern is with the meaning of what they want to say, not with the conventions of writing.

2. Authors' Circle helps students to see that writing is an ongoing process that may require revision to clarify meaning.

3. Authors' Circle also demonstrates the social nature of writing and helps students develop a sense of audience as they read what they have written to an audience and the audience responds to it.

4. Authors receive help on what they have written based on the audience's questions and responses. Authors also receive help on what is and is not working in their writing and what, if anything, they might consider doing next.

5. Authors do not revise during the circle, but later they consider privately the recommendations made and arrive at their own decisions regarding any changes in their writing. It is essential that this decision remain the author's responsibility so that the student maintains ownership of the piece. (Harste, Short, and Burke 1988, 221–22)

Variations

1. As students become more comfortable with the strategy, they should bring their concerns about the writing to the circle. (The Sample 1 Authors' Circle Comment Sheet that follows might be used when first introducing this strategy to students. The Sample 2 sheet could be used once students are familiar with the process and understand how peer feedback can help them improve certain aspects of the writing that they realize need improvement.)

2. Students who are listening to the piece might focus on the aspects of effective writing as a way to comment on the writing (e.g., organization, details, interesting opening, and so on).

3. The Fishbowl technique (see below for description) might be helpful when students are having difficulty with writing useful responses and questions. By observing other students who are providing feedback to a writer, they are able to see what types of comments are helpful and what types aren't.

4. Photocopying comments and questions from other classes and determining which ones help writers revise will provide students with models from which to develop an understanding of how to respond in future Authors' Circles.

5. Some students find it helpful to just listen to the piece first and then hear it a second time with an eye toward formulating questions. This allows them to enjoy the piece and to better understand the author's purpose and direction during the first hearing. On the second hearing, students can listen for parts of the writing that need details or were unclear.

Sample 1

Authors' Circle Comment Sheet

Author _____

Reactions by _____

Date _____

Memorable Moments

After hearing the piece of writing read aloud, what is the most memorable part for you? Why do you think this part stayed in your mind?

Questions

As a reader (listener), what do you not understand? Where could you use further information and/or details?

Sample 2

Authors' Circle Comment Sheet

Author _____

Comments by _____

Date _____

Author's Concerns

List the questions or concerns the author would like you to respond to.

What is your response to the author's concerns?

Memorable Moments

Record one sentence or portion of the writing that caught your attention. Briefly explain why you noticed this part.

Questions

What do you want to know more about, or what does the author need to consider when revising?

"What Do I Teach for 90 Minutes?" by Carol Porter © 2002 by NCTE.

Bookmarks

Bookmarks are small slips of blank paper that can be tucked into a book and used for writing responses to literature (Watson 1978). They are a strategy to help readers make meaning of a piece of literature. Written responses on Bookmarks can include, but are not limited to, the following: what a reader thinks is important in the piece, favorite parts, connections to the reader's personal experiences, questions about something in the piece that is not understood, something that the reader thinks is interesting about the piece, and predictions about where the text is headed. After several attempts with Bookmarks, students should work toward supporting the statements they are making in their writing. For example, when writing about their predictions, students should identify what from their experience or from the text led them to make each prediction. Students can star (*) selected comments on their Bookmarks to take to discussion.

Fishbowl

This strategy is used primarily when groups are discussing as a way for students to learn about group processes. One small group works together in the center of the room while the rest of the class forms a circle around this group and observes. The group in the center might be discussing a piece of literature, and the group on the outside could be observing the process—what types of interactions promote learning when discussing. Or the group on the outside might be listening to the content without being able to talk. In this case, they could be taking notes about comments they want to make once the small-group discussion has been completed. This strategy could also be used with Authors' Circle so that students can draw conclusions about the process and the types of questions that are helpful to a writer.

Focused Freewriting

Focused freewriting works the same way as freewriting except that students start with a specific topic. While writing, they may digress and interrupt their ideas, but eventually they should attempt to return to the topic.

- Focused freewriting can be a good way to record initial reactions to a piece of reading or a class discussion.

Variations

1. Define a concept. The teacher may use focused freewriting as a way for students to arrive at a definition of a concept or initial understanding of the unit question.

2. Students could respond to a quote written on the board or on an overhead from a piece of literature that the teacher or other students have chosen. Students then write about their interpretations, their personal connections, or how they think the quote represents the author's intent.

3. A focused freewrite might also address reactions to a poem.

Freewriting

Freewriting is connecting with a person's stream of consciousness—writing down whatever is going on in the mind at a particular time. To do this, the writer simply picks up a pen or pencil and writes continuously without stopping. Students might write about whatever they are thinking, feeling, or experiencing at the moment; what appears on the page may be words, phrases, or even doodles (Elbow and Belanoff 1989).

1. Freewriting is just a good first step of writing.

2. Freewriting takes advantage of the fact that our brains are always making meaning, seeking connections, creating stories and metaphors.

3. The teacher sets a time limit (usually five to fifteen minutes), and the student writes without pausing for that time period.

4. The aim of freewriting is not to produce "good" writing but to establish a writing fluency.

5. Freewriting may produce a single good sentence or paragraph worth saving, a piece for the middle of an assigned topic, or an idea for a piece of writing that the student can return to later.

Goal-Setting Conferences

When students finish their speeches or group presentations, complete a major piece of writing, or have responded in writing or in small group discussions over a period of time, the teacher can set aside time to talk about and record students' strengths as well as goals that should be set for future engagements in similar learning experiences. In this way, students can better focus on what they personally need to accomplish in order to produce high-quality work. Much like minilessons, discussing procedures for accomplishing these goals in a one-on-one setting helps students know what to do to meet their goals.

Once students know the purpose for goal-setting conferences and the criteria for effective work, they should be able to lead their own conferences by coming to the meeting with questions for the teacher and ideas for future work in reading, writing, and speaking. Students' personal goals can also be incorporated into grading rubrics, so that students are held accountable for accomplishing work specific to them.

Following are two forms and a number of questions for supporting goal setting and reflective self-evaluation.

Goal-Setting Form #1

Name _____ Date _____

Reading Goal(s):
    Steps I will take to accomplish the goal(s):

Writing Goals:
    Content:
    Steps I will take to accomplish the goal(s):

    Grammar/Mechanics:
    Steps I will take to accomplish the goal(s):

Speaking Goals:
    Formal:
    Steps I will take to accomplish the goal(s):

    Informal (Discussions):
    Steps I will take to accomplish the goal(s):

Goal-Setting Form #2

	Reading	Writing Content	Writing Grammar/Mechanics	Speaking Formal	Speaking Informal
Date: **Unit:**					
Problem I'm having					
Goal					
Steps I will take to accomplish this goal in English class					
How might I work on this goal in other classes?					

"Checking-In" Questions*

1. At what time during class were you most engaged as a learner?
2. At what time during class were you most distanced as a learner?
3. What was the most significant thing that happened to you as a learner this week?
4. What action did you find most puzzling or confusing?
5. What surprised you the most?

Other Questions*

- What have I learned this week about myself as a learner?
- What have I learned this week about my emotional responses to learning?
- What were the highest emotional moments in my learning activities this week?
- What were the lowest emotional moments in my learning activities this week?
- What learning tasks did I respond to most easily this week?
- What learning tasks gave me the greatest difficulties this week?
- What was the most significant thing that happened to me as a learner this week?
- What learning activity or emotional response most took me by surprise this week?
- Of everything I did this week in my learning, what would I do differently if I had to do it again?
- What do I feel proudest of in my learning activities this week?
- What do I feel most dissatisfied with in my learning activities this week?

*From *Becoming a Critically Reflective Teacher* by Stephen D. Brookfield

Graphic Organizers

As a reading strategy, Graphic Organizers assist learners in processing information before, during, and after reading. Graphic Organizers can also be used as a prewriting strategy to help organize thoughts and ideas for a piece of writing.

Two forms that Graphic Organizers can take are T-charts and clusters (see below for an example of each). Clustering in particular is a versatile strategy:

1. Clustering encourages students to write responses/reactions in order to generate ideas, form insights about the reading material, and create connections and relationships.

2. Students can utilize clustering for a variety of purposes: as an outline or list of subtopics the student can bring to literature discussion, as scaffolding that leads to issues you may want to focus on within a larger topic, as a guide to a group of issues related to one another, and as a way to identify or attach labels to ideas and people.

3. To demonstrate the use of this strategy, teachers should use it themselves when whole-class discussion leads to the consideration of many interrelated ideas.

T-Chart Graphic Organizer

Similarities	Differences

Questions:

Character Cluster

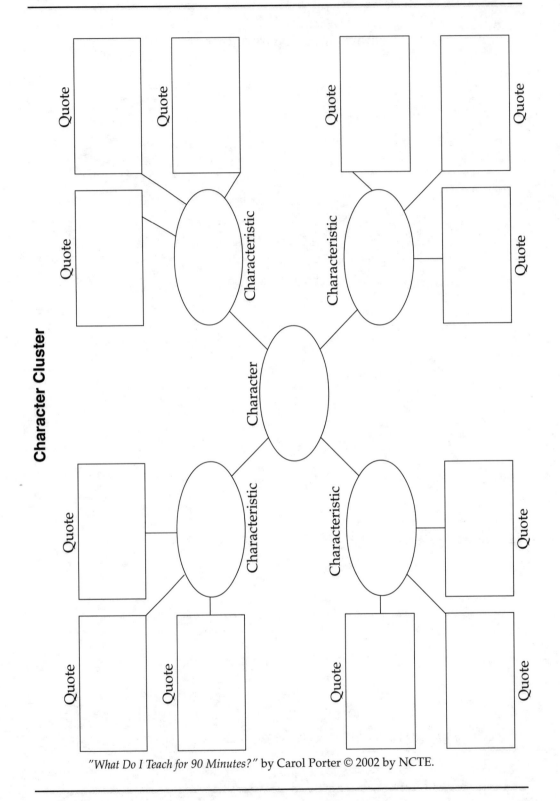

Inductive Analysis of Quality Materials

This is a strategy that can be used to create rubrics, grade sheets, or guides for written responses to literature, as well as for other types of writing, speeches, discussions, and/or projects. It requires that the students and teacher examine final products of the type that the students will be producing. Once quality standards have been determined through inductive analysis, these guides or grade sheets can be used by students while planning, drafting, and revising their work.

1. Provide students with samples of work similar to the types that they will be creating. Samples do not all have to be of high quality, since being able to see differences is helpful. (The choice of samples depends on what students need to analyze. For example, students might view video clips of literature discussions as a way to improve their interactions, or they might look at student samples of Written Conversation [see description below] in order to improve the quality of these types of responses to literature.)

2. Have students determine, in groups or individually, what they think was done well in the sample(s) and what areas they think need improvement. (The T-chart that appears at the end of this numbered list might be used for this purpose.)

3. Once students have generated lists, have them bring their ideas to the larger group and record these on newsprint or on a computer with LCD projection to an overhead screen. The teacher should have worked with one of the groups so that his/her ideas are included in the analysis. After everyone has shared, it is helpful to group similar ideas together into categories. (For example, for a discussion grade sheet, "Nonverbal Responses" and "Verbal Responses" might be two categories that emerge from the analysis.)

4. The teacher or student(s) then write(s) a rough draft guide sheet or grade sheet from this brainstormed list honoring as much of the students' language as possible.

5. On the following day, the rough draft is shared with the group (each student receives a copy) in order to gain ideas for revision.

6. Revisions are made to the document and then distributed to students for use throughout the remainder of the process. (For example, students have found that grade sheets for specific types of writing are helpful when seeking ideas for revision at Authors' Circle, and the student charts created for literature discussion have served as a reminder and a tool for reflection.)

T-Chart for Inductive Analysis

What did the writer/speaker do well?	What could the writer/speaker do to improve the response?

Jigsaw

Jigsaw is a method of dividing the material to be learned between students who then take responsibility for learning their part and teaching the rest of the class (Aronson, Stephan, Sikes, Blaney, and Snapp 1978). Most teachers have had the experience of really understanding something once they have to teach it. This strategy capitalizes on teaching others as a way to learn. When the materials are divided among groups of students, collaborative learning is highlighted both within and between groups. Finding a way for students to be responsible for the information that other groups are presenting is usually essential to the success of this strategy.

In the English classroom, different pieces by the same author can be divided among groups of students; in addition, different authors writing during the same time period can be studied by groups and presented to the class. Rather than giving a lecture on Romanticism, for example, a teacher could divide the various influences of the time period among groups for them to study and then teach the class.

KWL

Donna M. Ogle has written that, in order "to read well, we must access the knowledge we already have about the topic, or make it available appropriately so that comprehension can occur" (1986, p. 564). This strategy helps readers access what they *know* (K), determine what they *want* to learn (W), and recall what they did *learn* as a result of reading (L) (Ogle 1986).

Step K: "What I *know*"

Ogle presents this first step as involving "two levels of accessing prior knowledge. The first is a straightforward **brainstorming** of what the group knows about the topic for reading" (p. 565). The goal is to activate "whatever knowledge or structures the readers have that will help them interpret what they read." The second part of the brainstorming is to get students to think about "general **categories of information**" that might be found in the reading and then place the previously generated ideas into these categories.

Step W: "What do I *want* to learn?"

Ogle describes this step as follows: "As students take time to think about what they already know about the topic and the general categories of information that should be anticipated, questions emerge. Not all students agree on the same pieces of information; some information is conflicting, and some of the categories have had no particular information provided" (p. 566). Students should write questions that focus on what they want to learn. This portion of the strategy could be done with the entire class, and then students could individually list questions that are of interest to them.

Step L: "What I *learned*"

After completing the reading, students write down what they learned. They should "check their questions to determine [whether the text] dealt with [all of] their concerns" (p. 567). They should go to other texts to find answers to any questions that were not answered.

Most Important Word

In this strategy (Padak 1992), readers select what they believe to be the most important word in the text they have read. Readers must be able to explain the reason(s) why they think this particular word is the most important. After each student determines what he or she believes to be the most important word, discussion groups meet. Each person shares his or her choice and explains the reason(s) for choosing this particular word. After each person has shared and each word has been discussed, students should reconsider their word choice based upon the group discussion. Some students may change their word choice as a result of the discussion, while others may stick with their original word. Students should also explain their reasons for choosing the new word or sticking with their original choice. Groups can then discuss until they reach consensus on the most important word. These words can be shared with the class, along with the groups' reasons for their word choice.

Perspective Taking

Multiple interpretations can be constructed for the same text because of the many varying perspectives that each reader brings to the task. One way to highlight how this works is to return to a text that has been previously read and reread it from another perspective. After rereading the text, the selection can then be discussed with others who have taken alternative perspectives. Often, this is a strategy that facilitates discussion, because each reader comes to the table as an expert on the perspective that he or she took.

1. Read the text and discuss.

2. After discussion, have the class brainstorm various perspectives that others might bring to the reading of a text (e.g., artist, historian, scientist, environmentalist, immigrant, politician).

3. Have students choose a perspective to take and then reread the selection while attempting to think as the person they have chosen might think.

4. A writing-to-learn strategy could be used during and after the reading to examine the new ideas and interpretations that were gained, as well as the strategies that were used while reading.

5. Discussion can be set up in a variety of ways. For example, each person in the group may want to state an opinion from his or her chosen perspective to begin the discussion, or students could assume the role and anticipated personality of the type of person whose perspective they assumed.

6. The discussion of the literature should be followed with a process reflection so that readers can see how perspective taking alters meanings that are created.

Variations

1. Character roles and scenarios could be assigned prior to reading.

2. Perspective taking doesn't have to be limited to reading; it is a strategy that can also be used when students are watching a video or when they are writing.

Quote-Response

This strategy is similar to Most Important Word. Students select words, phrases, or sentences that catch their attention in a piece of literature. They then need to explain why they selected that particular passage and what the passage means to them.

1. As with Most Important Word, students need to explain the reason(s) for their choices.

2. Response journals with recorded quotes can serve as the impetus for small-group and/or whole-class discussion.

3. Students may also do a focused freewrite based on their choice of passage and/or based on group discussion.

Variation

Students may locate quotes to help them answer the unit question, analyze a character, or illustrate contrasting points of view.

Quote-Response

Words, phrases, or sentences that caught my attention (include p. #):

Why I selected the above passage, and what the passage means to me:

Freewrite:

ReQuest: Reciprocal Questioning

Asking questions is something good readers do, yet many adolescent readers think it is something that only poor readers do. This strategy promotes questioning, which in turn helps readers to make predictions, and supports comprehension (adapted from Manzo 1969). The students should read a small portion of text knowing that when they are finished they will be asking the teacher questions. Students' questions in this strategy can fall into four categories: "school questions" (e.g., What is the author's purpose?), recall questions (e.g., Where was the first scene in the story set?), response questions (e.g., What portion of the essay or story did you like best?), and "real" questions (e.g., Why would someone write this type of essay?) (Manzo 1969, 43). In answering the questions, teachers can also share their reading and thinking processes. After answering a question, the teacher then asks the student a question, modeling, as much as possible, the response and "real" types of questions. In this way, students can both experience success and be pushed to predict where the text might go next. Students and the teacher continue with reciprocal questioning until the text is completed or until enough of the text is understood so that students can finish the text independently.

Save the Last Word for Me

The unique experiences and knowledge that each reader brings to the text influence the meaning that he or she creates in reading it. This strategy highlights and encourages the multiple interpretations that can be elicited by a text (Burke in Harste, Short, and Burke 1988). Often, students have been taught that they should be looking for a single interpretation or, in the case of struggling readers, that other students know the "right" interpretation. In contrast, "Save the Last Word for Me demonstrates to them that all readers work at constructing their own interpretations of what they read through relating their background experiences to the text as well as through discussing the text with other readers" (332).

Much like Most Important Word and Quote-Response, students write a word, phrase, or quote on an index card after reading a text or portion of a text. Their reasons for choosing the word, phrase, or quote are listed on the back of the card, along with the meaning they constructed from that portion of the text. Students can create more than one card. If they do, they should put these in order beginning with those they most want to discuss. In small groups, students read their word, phrase, or quote, and other group members react by stating what meaning they make and what reactions they have. After each member of the group responds, the student who wrote the card has the last word by sharing information from the back of the card and responding to the comments that others in the group made. Discussion continues in this manner until all students have shared at least one card. This strategy for discussion can also be used with Sketch to Stretch (see below), where students might create a symbol depicting a character, for example, and then work in groups to arrive at meanings. They would then let the author of the sketch have the last word.

Say Something

Partners silently read the same piece of literature to a predetermined stopping point (page or chapter) and then discuss with each other whatever they think is important about the piece (Harste, Short, and Burke 1988). Comments may include favorite parts, questions about something in the piece that was not understood, and/or something that one or both partners found interesting. They can discuss thoughts about a life experience that can be connected with the piece or predictions about what may happen next. Students may also want to share what they were thinking about while reading and what they did when they had a question or did not understand something in the text. Reading and discussing should continue in the same way until readers reach the end of the story or novel.

1. Teachers should encourage risk taking and allow students to construct their own meanings for a given piece of literature. The risks taken with Say Something are less threatening because comments are made to one other peer rather than to the entire class.

2. Say Something allows students to bounce ideas and interpretations off one another, ask questions, and make confirmations on a one-to-one basis.

3. The nature of the discussion between partners can be shared with the rest of the class to promote a whole-class literature discussion.

4. The teacher may alternate partners throughout the course of reading a book in order to discuss one-on-one with each member of the class.

5. Say Something can be used while reading a short story, novel, or other type of text aloud.

Sketch to Stretch

Taking the ideas from one sign system (in an English classroom, this usually means written and spoken language) and representing it in another is the basic idea behind sketch to stretch. Essentially, learners are taking ideas beyond a literal understanding as they make interpretations in their drawings, because they are thinking symbolically and metaphorically (Harste, Short, and Burke 1988).

To introduce the strategy, it is helpful to explain to students that they should draw a sketch of what the reading selection meant to them or what they made of the reading. After time is given for sketching, students should share their pieces in groups, with other students telling what they think the artist is trying to say. Once all group members have described their interpretation of the sketch, the artist gets to have the "last word." Sharing continues in this way until all group members have shared their sketches. The sketches can be compiled into a class book, or displayed around the room. Students should be encouraged to use this strategy as an alternative to writing, since the interpretations and meanings that emerge from using the language of visual representation are often different from what can be expressed in words.

Speakers' Circle

Speakers' Circle is similar to Authors' Circle because speakers use this strategy to get ideas for revising their oral presentations or speeches. The same procedures for sharing and providing feedback that are used in Authors' Circle are used with Speakers' Circle. After revising the content of the presentation, students return to the circle to gain feedback on their revisions and delivery. Students may also want to videotape their speech and analyze it with the group. Revising, rehearsing, and returning to Speakers' Circle may be repeated several times before delivering the speech in its "final draft" form.

Written Conversation

Partners using this strategy "talk" about literature by carrying on a conversation with each other in writing (Harste, Short, and Burke 1988). After reading a predetermined portion of the text, readers address their responses to their partner. The two then exchange their notes and respond to each other's writing, after which the initial piece, along with the partner's response, is returned to the original writer. The content of the Written Conversation should be directed toward trying to make meaning of the piece of literature through questions, comments, discussion of likes/dislikes, and making connections with life experiences.

Appendix E: Curriculum Map

The following calendar progression maps the sophomore curriculum on a 4x4 block schedule. (See sample unit plan in Chapter 3 [Figure 3].)

August

Sunday	Monday	Tuesday	Wednesday	Thursday	Friday	Saturday
		1st	2nd	3rd	4th	5th
6th	7th	8th	9th	10th	11th	12th
13th	14th	15th	16th Term 1 begins	17th	18th	19th
20th	21st	22nd	23rd	24th	25th	26th
27th	28th	29th	30th	31st		

September

Sunday	Monday	Tuesday	Wednesday	Thursday	Friday	Saturday
					1st	2nd
3rd	4th	5th	6th Personal narrative	7th	8th	9th
10th	11th	12th	13th	14th	15th Finish novel	16th
17th	18th	19th	20th	21st Persuasive essay	22nd	23rd
24th	25th	26th	27th	28th	29th	30th

October

Sunday	Monday	Tuesday	Wednesday	Thursday	Friday	Saturday
1st	2nd Finish free-choice novel	3rd	4th	5th	6th Editorial	7th
8th	9th	10th	11th Portfolio	12th	13th Unit question essay	14th
15th	16th Exams, informative speeches	17th Exams, informative speeches	18th Professional Development Day	19th Term 2 begins	20th	21st
22nd	23rd	24th	25th	26th	27th	28th
29th	30th	31st				

November

Sunday	Monday	Tuesday	Wednesday	Thursday	Friday	Saturday
			1st	2nd	3rd Finish play	4th
5th	6th	7th	8th	9th	10th Character analysis	11th
12th	13th	14th	15th	16th	17th	18th
19th	20th	21st	22nd Finish novel	23rd	24th	25th
26th	27th	28th	29th	30th		

December

Sunday	Monday	Tuesday	Wednesday	Thursday	Friday	Saturday
					1st	2nd
3rd	4th	5th Multigenre research papers	6th	7th	8th	9th
10th	11th	12th	13th	14th	15th Multigenre portfolios	16th
17th	18th	19th	20th Finals, research presentations	21st Finals, research presentations	22nd	23rd
24th	25th	26th	27th	28th	29th	30th
31st						

Appendix F: Sample Unit (Expressions: Literature and the Arts)

Table of Contents

Questions and Answers about Expressions: Literature and the Arts

Why was this course written?

In October, student representatives from each of the junior English sections met with English teachers to talk about their learning experiences, interests, and needs with regard to senior course offerings. These students had completed two years in detracked, learner-centered English classes at Mundelein High School and were currently in the first semester of their junior year. Many of the students who attended this session had experienced success in traditional English programs in various

---

This unit was written by Mundelein High School teachers Robert Machak, Brad Swanson, and Ed Solis. (Robert Machak is now at Field Middle School in Northbrook, Illinois, and Brad Swanson is now at Maine Township High School West in Des Plaines, Illinois.) The unit is reprinted here by permission of the authors.

feeder schools and were still adjusting to the "new way of doing things," while other students had experienced success at Mundelein for the first time in their school careers. One idea that came from this teacher-student discussion was a class that would be designed in a way that student could learn how to write the type of interpretative and critical analysis papers that colleges might require while they were engaged in the study of literature and the expressive and visual arts.

How does this course connect to what the students have previously studied?

The strategies that students will use (e.g., Authors' Circle, literature discussions) to help them in their understanding and development of ideas are the ones they have used in previous English courses. Since students have had considerable experience in applying these strategies to many different learning situations, the teacher will be supporting their independent and personalized application of strategies.

Like previous English courses, this course is structured around inquiry and begins with the teacher-generated question "What Is Expression?" Within the first weeks of instruction, the students and teacher should be generating their own individual inquiry questions that will begin to guide and shape the directions that the class as a whole, and students individually, will take in their learning. As questions become more narrowly focused and individualized, students will begin an I-Search exploration.

What makes this course different from other English courses?

In previous English units, core resources were identified, and students and teachers learned from those materials before moving into personal areas of inquiry. The curriculum for this course is designed with an open-ended format in which students negotiate the content from the beginning. Two types of "resource clusters" have been developed: one type addressing a theme (e.g., "Pain and Loss") and the other addressing a historical period (e.g., the Victorian era). (Four sample clusters are included near the end of this appendix.) During the first term, each class will choose a themed or historical cluster identifying some core materials and suggesting other possibilities. As questions and interests surface, the class will complete the cluster by choosing pieces of literature, film, art, and music which will help them answer the questions and support their interests. The combination of what they have learned about the content and what they have learned about the "nuts and bolts" of each medium will help them decide what they might want to investigate in the second half of the term. By the end of the first unit, each student will begin drafting his or her personal cluster that will guide much of the learning in the second unit and/or second nine weeks.

Assessment will be more multifaceted in this course. For example, a student might choose to create a video presentation on the hero figures depicted in various literary and artistic formats. Not only would the student be examining and analyzing materials from a variety of sources, but he or she would also be incorporating a variety of forms of expression in the final presentation.

How were the core materials chosen?

Choosing from among the thousands of works in each of the media is not a simple task, but we found that if we asked ourselves several questions about materials, the decisions were a little easier. The first question, "What materials will best help students in reaching the outcomes?" helped us to generate a long list of materials. From this list we eliminated literature materials based on the answer to the second question, "What might students read in World Literature or English Literature?" We added additional titles after asking ourselves, "What materials have been tried in a number of different media?" (e.g., *Romeo and Juliet* and *West Side Story*). We also considered materials in relation to the theme and time-period clusters that were chosen. Finally, we tried to strike a delicate balance between choosing some of the "classics" that some students said they wanted to read prior to college and, at the same time, considering the current needs, abilities, and interests of all students.

What should students be able to do when they finish this class?

Generally, students should be able to demonstrate an understanding of each of the outcomes listed in the outcomes section of the units. In addition to these goals, we thought it was important to just begin to touch the surface of some of the "classics" within each of the media while giving students a basis for analysis and interpretation of works in each medium. Instead of students saying simply, "This is stupid [or boring, or dumb]," they should be able to support their opinions about different forms of expressions using terms appropriate to each. In addition, students will continue to develop skills and strategies that will support them in future learning situations. The second unit is structured in such a way that students will be responsible for planning their independent investigations.

How will the final demonstration (assessment) be graded?

Students will need to show their abilities in relation to each of the out-comes. It is possible that the students and teacher can create a project that displays all of the outcomes, but some students might need to cre-ate multiple projects in order to accomplish each of the outcomes.

An Inductive Analysis of Quality Materials strategy will be used to create grade sheets while the project is being planned. This strategy requires that students and their teacher examine projects of high qual-ity that are similar to the ones being planned, in order to determine the categories that will be graded and the point values for each. This grade sheet can then be used as a guide by students while working on the project.

Student Feedback Regarding Junior Curriculum

(Rough Draft Notes from 5/17/95)

Students Attending: Ray M., Keith M., Tim M., Heather S., Lynda S., Andrea C., Jim K., Tony L., Jason K., Eddie B., Sandra G., Cristina G., Dan H., Sue G., Heather M., Debbie W., and Glenn D.

- Discussions are beginning to work for most students. They are beginning to find that talking about their reading helps them to understand how to write better responses.
- All students thought the core novels should remain in the cur-riculum.
- Students who read plays liked them.
- Students who listened to poetry on records or tapes enjoyed this format.
- Poetry presentations done in several classes were a highlight. Some possible suggestions for these presentations were author studies, themes, and time periods.
- Students thought it was important to analyze poetry in relation to the unit question.
- Some students thought too much time was spent on one unit question, some thought it was the right amount, others didn't know the unit question, and still others suggested that the ques-tion be "dressed up." (To them, "dressing up" might mean ex-amining roles, rights, privileges, and responsibilities, or it might involve having students develop a personalized version of the question during a portion of the unit, or having students find their own angle in relation to the question.)

- Some students reported that their teachers had tried individual editing conferences in which they focused on grammar and punctuation. They wanted more of this. They saw the need for more grammar lessons to help them improve these aspects of their writing.

- The students said that Authors' Circles don't work when students are not given enough time both inside and outside of class to use them. Students said that they thought Authors' Circles need to be valued by the teacher. Some students still don't know how to make appropriate and helpful comments during Authors' Circle.

- Students believe that more speaking opportunities should be offered.

- Use of quotes and use of in-text citations are not fully understood by some students.

- Some students expressed frustration with assumptions that students can write an effective thesis and conclusion. (They said that if they can't do it, it's not because they don't want to—they probably need individual help.)

- Students thought there could be more coordination of strategies and projects with U.S. History. Could we coordinate projects with U.S. History?

- Students said they liked the unit on values. Some said that they liked picking a decade and looking at how the values from that decade have influenced their lives. (I think this was a speech in one teacher's class.)

- They said there was a sharp contrast between the sophomore questions and the junior questions. They said that the sophomore questions were too direct and obvious and that students need to personalize the question. In contrast, the junior questions meant something to them once they answered them.

- Some students said that they didn't like role-playing.

- One group of students said that they really liked acting out the court scene in *To Kill A Mockingbird*.

- Students want to do more with song lyrics and relate them to the unit question.

- Students who were in classes that did a free-choice novel thought that should be repeated.

- Some students mentioned a chart they used in relation to poetry interpretation that they found helpful for studying symbolism.

- Students believe that by junior year they have written too many reflection letters to the teacher.

- Responses to literature—not every chapter, maybe every three to five chapters. They said that responding to every chapter was busy work and we need to figure out how students can respond to help them understand.

- Some students used self-stick notes to mark areas for discussion during and after reading and thought that was a helpful strategy.

- Discussions help for understanding, if students are taking them seriously. Students thought we should be videotaping their discussions.

Annotated Bibliography of Materials to Support the Expressions Curriculum

Baker, Beverly. "A 'Novel' Approach to the Classics Relating Art and Literature." Pp. 11–13 in *Literature—News That Stays News: Fresh Approaches to the Classics,* ed. Candy Carter. Urbana, Ill.: National Council of Teachers of English, 1986.

> Describes an activity for using art in the English classroom; gives titles of artwork and novels used.

Barber, David W. *Bach, Beethoven, and the Boys: Music History as It Ought to Be Taught.* Toronto: Sound and Vision, 1986.

> Offers a humorous, easy-to-read guide to the lives of several famous composers.

———. *When the Fat Lady Sings: Opera History as It Ought to Be Taught.* Toronto: Sound and Vision, 1990.

> Presents an informative, easy-to-read guide for beginners in classical music. Gives information on specific composers and synopses of famous operas.

Boggs, Joseph M. *The Art of Watching Films: A Guide to Film Analysis.* Menlo Park, Calif.: Benjamin/Cummings, 1978.

> Provides detailed discussion of the importance of the musical score of a film. An excellent chapter on film analysis.

Bone, Jan, and Ron Johnson. *Understanding the Film: An Introduction to Film Appreciation.* 4th ed. Lincolnwood, Ill.: National Textbook Co., 1991.

> Includes a chapter on film techniques with specific examples and illustrations; is useful for building a vocabulary for film discussion.

Campbell, Joseph. *The Hero with a Thousand Faces.* Princeton, N.J.: Princeton University Press, 1949.

> Outlines the three stages of any heroic adventure story. This framework should facilitate discussion across genres and media.

Cavitch, David. *Life Studies: A Thematic Reader.* New York: St. Martin's Press, 1983.

Includes short stories, poems, and essays grouped in themes: self-images, family ties, group pictures, possessions, love and longings, and dilemmas. The table of contents contains short descriptions of each work.

Fulwiler, Toby, and the NCTE Commission on Composition. "Guidelines for Using Journals in School Settings." Pp. 5–18 in *The Journal Book*, ed. Toby Fulwiler. Portsmouth, N.H.: Boynton/Cook, 1987.

NCTE document which supports the value of journal writing as both a learning and a relationship-building strategy.

Gammond, Peter. *The Harmony Illustrated Encyclopedia of Classical Music*. New York: Harmony Books, 1988.

Provides technical information in dictionary form; analyzes each element's (i.e., composer's, instrument's) role in creating a piece of music.

Goodson, F. Todd. "Reading and Writing across Genres: Textual Form and Social Action in the High School." *Journal of Reading* 38.1 (1994): 6–12.

Discusses the benefits derived through allowing student choice and variety both in the types of reading materials selected and in the kinds of activities associated with them.

Huss, Roy, and Norman Silverstein. *The Film Experience: Elements of Motion Picture Art*. New York: Harper & Row, 1968.

Includes an insightful chapter on teaching students how to analyze cinematic theme through a variety of devices.

Masterworks of Art. Poster set. Madison, Wis.: Knowledge Unlimited, Inc. (http://thekustore.com/kucatalog.cgi/AP9W?U6tUTuaf;;24)

Set of eight laminated posters accompanied by biographical information on each artist (Cassatt, da Vinci, Matisse, Picasso, Rembrandt, Stuart, Toulouse-Latrec, van Gogh).

Medway, Peter. "Logs for Learning." Pp. 64–76 in *The Journal Book*, ed. Toby Fulwiler. Portsmouth, N.H.: Boynton/Cook, 1987.

Specific examples are given to show how journals helped one social studies teacher and his students move beyond "language" and into "understanding."

Monaco, James. *How to Read a Film: The Art, Technology, Language, History, and Theory of Film and Media*. New York: Oxford University Press, 1977.

Includes a difficult but helpful chapter on the signs and syntax used in film. Gets past the "whats" for a very detailed description of the "whys."

O'Connor, John E., and Martin A. Jackson, eds. *American History/American Film: Interpreting the Hollywood Image*. New York: Ungar, 1979.

Table of contents is arranged thematically and provides examples of movies which place specific films in some important historical context related to the themes (e.g., Cold War films). This could serve as a guide for student-generated units.

Peary, Gerald, and Roger Shatzkin, eds. *The Modern American Novel and the Movies.* New York: Ungar, 1978.

> Includes reviews that compare films to specific pieces of literature, focusing on changes from book to movie version.

Presidential Task Force on Psychology in Education and the American Psychological Association. *Learner-Centered Psychological Principles: Guidelines for School Redesign and Reform.* Denver, Colo.: McREL, 1993.

> This document guided the Expressions course's learner-centered philosophy.

Sullivan, Barbara. "Self-Images." *Chicago Tribune* (23 September 1994): 5.1, 5.2.

> Describes a poetry-writing activity based on student-taken photographs.

Visions of Light: The Art of Cinematography. Written and directed by Todd McCarthy. Beverly Hills, Calif.: CBS/Fox Video, 1994.

> Videotape which uses rare and current clips to show lighting and camera-angle techniques used to create or enhance meaning in a film.

Walsh, Michael. *Who's Afraid of Classical Music?* New York: Simon & Schuster, 1989.

> This beginner's guide to appreciating classical music includes discussion of how to listen to an opera, symphony, or concerto.

Wiggins, Grant. "Creating a Thought-Provoking Curriculum: Lessons from Whodunits and Others." *American Educator* 11.4 (1987): 10–17.

> Discusses the philosophy behind the creation of an inquiry-based curriculum, as well as the impetus for the search for more meaningful assessments.

Zaret, Esther. "The Uncertainty Principle in Curriculum Planning." *Theory into Practice* 25.1 (1986): 46–52.

> Addresses the importance of building in "unplanned time" in curriculum planning. The author advocates taking meaningful class discussion where students, not teachers, want it to go. Zaret argues that such discussions cannot be planned, nor should they be discounted in the curriculum. Provided the basis for deciding to have students develop their own unit with choices of resources used.

Mundelein High School Student Goals for Communication Arts

Students are:

- gaining insights into themselves and others by reading the classics as well as lesser-known works and contemporary literature;
- seeing information from a variety of sources as a way of creating meaning for themselves;

- using reading, writing, speaking, and listening for learning and interacting with others;
- interpreting ideas and language beyond the literal level by becoming active inquirers.

Mundelein High School Communication Arts Philosophy Statement

Reading, writing, speaking, listening, and thinking are essential for learning. These literate abilities are developed in an environment that supports risk taking, values differences, promotes inquiry, and encourages purposeful interactions. The process of enhancing literacy should center on the learner and reflect current knowledge about language development and learning theory. The Authoring Cycle is a model that can provide a curricular and instructional framework that is learner-centered by connecting to and moving from the learner's life experiences. Harste, Short, and Burke (1988) use authoring to describe the process of creating meaning, something that occurs not just when learners are writing but also when they're authoring ideas while reading, sketching, observing, discussing, acting, and so on. The Authoring Cycle process draws upon strategies that learners use while making connections to life experiences; engaging in uninterrupted time for reading writing, drawing, and so on; exploring meaning making with others; reflecting and revising; presenting and sharing meaning with others; examining the ways meaning is constructed and expressed in different sign systems; and using the questions and connections made while engaged in the process to determine new directions for learning. (A number of these activities are discussed in the chapter titled "An Authoring Cycle Model of Curriculum" in Short and Burke's *Creating Curriculum* [1991].)

What do we believe about curriculum?

Curriculum:

- serves as an organizing framework for the teacher;
- is a transaction between teacher, students, and content;
- is a well-revised document, but not a final draft;
- needs to be learner-centered;
- is a complex set of processes preserved on paper (paper curriculum) and enacted in the classroom (enacted curriculum). (This last descriptor is drawn from Short and Burke 1991.)

What do we believe about learning?

Learning:

- can't occur unless connections are made with what is known;
- is enhanced and supported through interaction;
- is acquired through reading, writing, listening, speaking, and thinking, as well as through nonverbal kinds of doing, e.g., playing the violin or dribbling a basketball;
- is supported in an environment that is accepting of individual differences.

Therefore the learner needs to be active, engaged, and willing and able to take risks.

What do we believe about instruction?

Instruction:

- should mirror beliefs about learning;
- evolves from where the learner is;
- is the connection between the learner and content;
- needs to be learner-centered, not teacher-centered.

What do we believe about content?

Content:

- is the vehicle for exploring areas of inquiry;
- is fluid and determined by the learner's needs;
- supports goals and outcomes;
- is accountable to measurable outcomes.

What do we believe about assessment?

Assessment:

- should inform instruction;
- needs to be a tool for learning, rather than the end product of learning;
- should involve learners in identifying what they can do, determining the strategies that support learning, and setting goals for future experiences;
- should specify standards, but this should not be the exclusive measure; development of the individual is of equal importance.

Senior English: Course Goals and Outcomes

1.0   Students are continuing to expand and refine their own learning processes through language experiences by

  1.1   evaluating situations for appropriate communication styles and formats;

  1.2   analyzing experiences and adapting strategies that are most effective in supporting learning;

  1.3   incorporating ideas, information, and strategies across various content areas;

  1.4   developing a repertoire of strategies to support self-directed learning.

2.0   Students are valuing the interactive nature of learning by

  2.1   modeling attitudes and behaviors of an effective group member;

  2.2   providing effective feedback to peers during shared writing and literature discussions;

  2.3   evaluating the collaborative situation and altering the group's interactions to achieve purposes;

  2.4   demonstrating an appreciation of differences in opinions.

3.0   Students are applying critical-thinking and problem-solving skills when

  3.1   engaging in active, purposeful inquiry to expand their knowledge;

  3.2   generating questions and predictions and giving rationales before, during, and after a variety of language experiences;

  3.3   drawing inferences appropriate to achieving a full understanding of the text;

  3.4   using specific information or reasons to support personal interpretations of language experiences (i.e., supporting written and oral opinions with evidence that meets a standard);

  3.5   integrating information from print and nonprint sources;

  3.6   incorporating inquiry as an integral part of the learning process;

  3.7   identifying, planning, and executing projects;

  3.8   applying genre-based criteria to support personal evaluation of various forms of expression.

4.0   Students are continuing to refine their abilities to communicate effectively by

  4.1   generating and presenting original thoughts and ideas;

  4.2   exploring alternative modes of expression (within

Vygotsky's zone of proximal development) for displaying understanding;

4.3 selecting the most effective mode of expression (personally and contextually) to demonstrate understanding;

4.4 analyzing and critiquing the various ideas in forms of expression (e.g., abstract, surreal, impressionistic);

4.5 developing and maintaining a focus using specific information or reasons to support and elaborate the thesis;

4.6 organizing ideas clearly, concisely, and logically for the appropriate format;

4.7 using conventions of Standard English;

4.8 incorporating revision and editing strategies.

5.0 Students are emerging as self-directed learners when

5.1 using inquiry as the impetus for knowledge;

5.2 using reflection to make decisions about content, process, and purpose;

5.3 linking new information with existing knowledge in meaningful ways.

Course Description

EXPRESSIONS: LITERATURE AND THE ARTS ($\frac{1}{2}$ Credit)   Senior
Prerequisite: English 3
After studying various authors, social issues, and genres through literature, students will design their own search as a way to deepen their understanding of a particular area of interest or inquiry. Although critical analysis of literature is the emphasis of the course, several media of expression, such as film, television, art, dance, and music, will be integrated to provide opportunities for students to develop critical literacy/ thinking across media.

Core Unit Plan—First Term
"What is Expression?"

Learning Outcomes	Demonstrations of Learning/Assessment	Strategies	Resources
Students are 1-a critiquing various forms of expression and considering the parameters of and influences on the various forms: ▪ parameters—the structures of each form (e.g., music, written story, film, painting); ▪ limitations—e.g., painting is only 2-D, in film it's difficult to express first-person pt. of view, in drama and movies less opportunity to give background information; ▪ influences—e.g., censorship, society, business/industry, government, other products of same medium, directors/authors influenced by others in the same profession. 1-b supporting generalizations about various forms of expression using appropriate literary devices: ▪ vocabulary associated with each; ▪ point of view. 1-c analyzing the commonalities of various forms of expression: ▪ universal conflicts; ▪ themes; ▪ literary devices; ▪ treatment of same subject matter. 1-d using specific information to support personal interpretations of various forms of expression: ▪ theme; ▪ genre (e.g. "This is what film says about heroes."); ▪ given three versions of the same "story," which is the most effective, and why? 1-e engaging in active, purposeful inquiry to expand their knowledge about various forms of expression.	Students will demonstrate their emerging abilities and understandings of each of the outcomes through: ▪ discussion; ▪ journal writing; ▪ focused freewrites; ▪ learning logs; ▪ Save the Last Word for Me. By the end of this unit, students will demonstrate their abilities and their understandings of each of the outcomes in one or more of the following formats: ▪ video presentation (e.g., documentary, talk show); ▪ literary criticism; ▪ film review; ▪ music video; ▪ discussion/panel presentation; ▪ thematic portfolio or annotated scrapbook. (Students might design their own demonstration with teacher approval.)	Authors' Circle Focused freewrites Gardner's multiple intelligences Learning log Literature discussion Quote-Response journal Peer editing ReQuest Save the Last Word for Me Self-editing Speakers' Circle	**Video** ▪ *Visions of Light* (illustration of cinematographic techniques) ▪ *Citizen Kane* (Orson Welles) **Poetry/Art** ▪ "Goya" (Andrei Voznesensky) See other specific works listed in the resource clusters following the Unit Plan grids (i.e., "Anger and Fear," "Pain and Loss," "Hope and Joy," and "The Victorian Age").

Core Unit Plan—Second Term
"Student-Generated Question"

Learning Outcomes	Demonstrations of Learning/Assessment	Strategies	Resources
Students are 2-a critiquing various forms of expression and considering the parameters of and influences on the various forms: ■ parameters—the structures of each form (e.g., music, written story, film, painting); ■ limitations—e.g., painting is only 2-D, in film it's difficult to express first-person pt. of view, in drama and movies less opportunity to give background information; ■ influences—e.g., censorship, society, business/industry, government, other products of same medium, directors/authors influenced by others in the same profession. 2-b supporting generalizations about various forms of expression using appropriate literary devices: ■ vocabulary associated with each; ■ point of view. 2-c analyzing the commonalities of various forms of expression: ■ universal conflicts; ■ themes; ■ literary devices; ■ treatment of same subject matter. 2-d using specific information to support personal interpretations of various forms of expression: ■ theme; ■ genre (e.g. "This is what film says about heroes."); ■ given three versions of the same "story," which is the most effective, and why? 2-e engaging in active, purposeful inquiry to expand their knowledge about various forms of expression.	By the end of this unit, students will demonstrate their abilities and their understandings of each of the outcomes in one or more of the following formats: ■ video presentation (e.g., documentary, talk show); ■ literary criticism; ■ film review; ■ music video; ■ discussion/panel presentation; ■ thematic portfolio or annotated scrapbook. (Students might design their own demonstration with teacher approval.)	Authors' Circle Focused freewrites Gardner's multiple intelligences Learning log Literature discussion Quote-Response journal Peer editing ReQuest Save the Last Word for Me Self-editing Speakers' Circle	Student-selected resources related to the inquiry question for which he or she is seeking an answer.

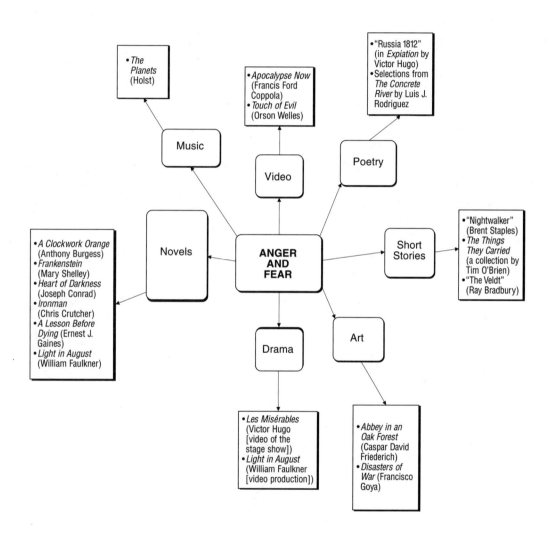

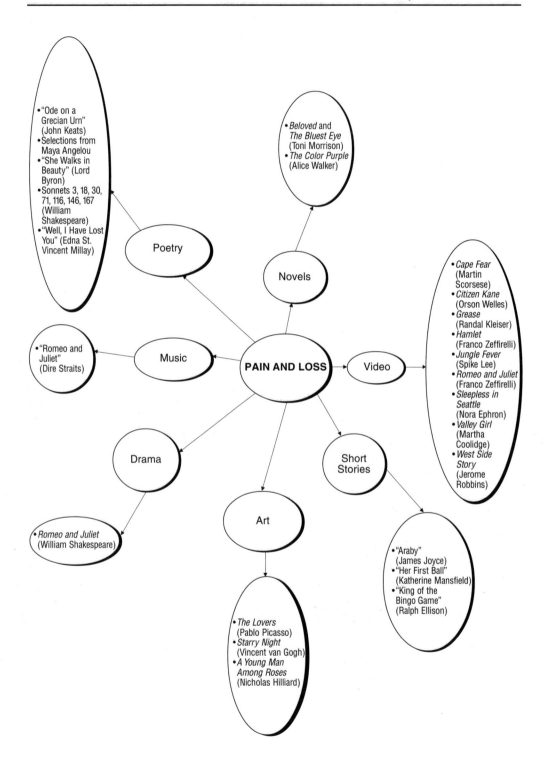

PAIN AND LOSS

Poetry
• "Ode on a Grecian Urn" (John Keats)
• Selections from Maya Angelou
• "She Walks in Beauty" (Lord Byron)
• Sonnets 3, 18, 30, 71, 116, 146, 167 (William Shakespeare)
• "Well, I Have Lost You" (Edna St. Vincent Millay)

Novels
• *Beloved* and *The Bluest Eye* (Toni Morrison)
• *The Color Purple* (Alice Walker)

Music
• "Romeo and Juliet" (Dire Straits)

Video
• *Cape Fear* (Martin Scorsese)
• *Citizen Kane* (Orson Welles)
• *Grease* (Randal Kleiser)
• *Hamlet* (Franco Zeffirelli)
• *Jungle Fever* (Spike Lee)
• *Romeo and Juliet* (Franco Zeffirelli)
• *Sleepless in Seattle* (Nora Ephron)
• *Valley Girl* (Martha Coolidge)
• *West Side Story* (Jerome Robbins)

Drama
• *Romeo and Juliet* (William Shakespeare)

Short Stories
• "Araby" (James Joyce)
• "Her First Ball" (Katherine Mansfield)
• "King of the Bingo Game" (Ralph Ellison)

Art
• *The Lovers* (Pablo Picasso)
• *Starry Night* (Vincent van Gogh)
• *A Young Man Among Roses* (Nicholas Hilliard)

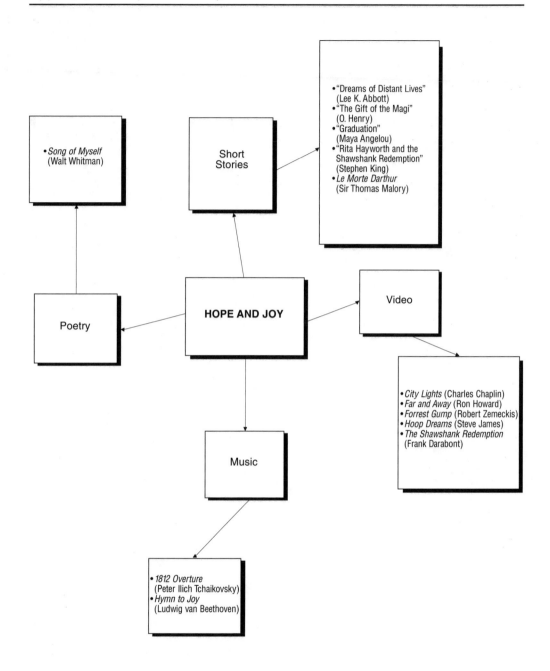

Short Stories
- "Dreams of Distant Lives" (Lee K. Abbott)
- "The Gift of the Magi" (O. Henry)
- "Graduation" (Maya Angelou)
- "Rita Hayworth and the Shawshank Redemption" (Stephen King)
- *Le Morte Darthur* (Sir Thomas Malory)

Poetry
- *Song of Myself* (Walt Whitman)

HOPE AND JOY

Video
- *City Lights* (Charles Chaplin)
- *Far and Away* (Ron Howard)
- *Forrest Gump* (Robert Zemeckis)
- *Hoop Dreams* (Steve James)
- *The Shawshank Redemption* (Frank Darabont)

Music
- *1812 Overture* (Peter Ilich Tchaikovsky)
- *Hymn to Joy* (Ludwig van Beethoven)

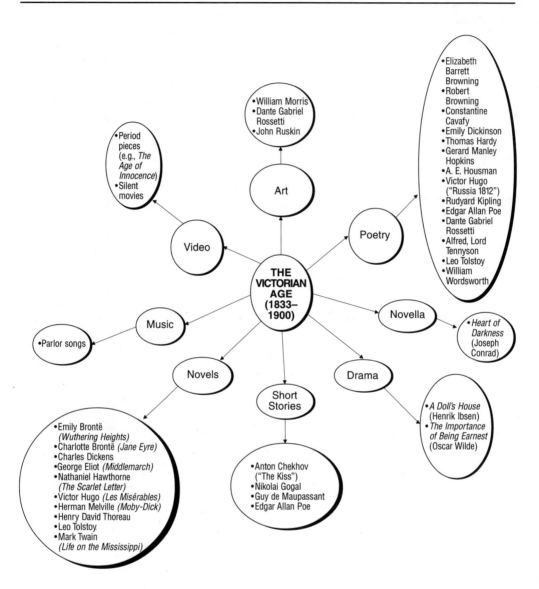

Community-Building Activities Connected to Unit Question

How do people express themselves?

- Have students work in small groups to brainstorm various ways in which people express themselves.
- Groups might be assigned general categories within which to generate more specific ideas.
- Some categories might include:
  - gestures
  - idioms/slogans
  - clothing
  - music
  - famous people
- Have small groups share with the larger group.
- Have students freewrite or make a journal entry connected with the ideas that were shared. (Students may also want to write about the ways in which they express themselves.)

Music and/or Video

- Play conflicting moods and/or images.
- Discuss.
- Write.

Poetry Sort

- Place poetry selections from a wide variety of authors and themes in packets or envelopes.
- Have students work in small groups to identify themes found in the poetry included in their packet.
- Have groups share the themes they identified and record these for the class to see.
- Discuss commonalities and "spin-offs" related to the themes students found in the poems.
- Have each group share a favorite poem with the larger group.

Appendix G: Advancement Center Forms

Advancement Center Student Admittance/Activity Sheet

Teacher signature _____ Time _____
Student(s) _____ Period _____ Date _____
_____
Predicted amount of time required in Advancement Center _____

Student/Teacher Activity

_____ Guide through attached assignment
_____ Plan and write rough draft
_____ Listen to speech/provide feedback
_____ Videotape speech/presentation
_____ Participate in small group discussion (videotape___yes___no)
_____ View videotape/assist in goal setting
_____ View small-group discussion videotape and analyze with
     students
_____ Participate in Authors' Circle:
     _____ please work with students
     _____ students can work on their own

All the above activities require students to come to the Advancement Center with:

    1. current goal sheet

    2. assignment prompt

    3. assignment grading criteria

_____ Work on computer
_____ Work with enrichment materials
     Thematic unit: _____
_____ Choose free-choice novel
     Thematic unit: _____
_____ Listen to book on tape
_____ Research materials needed
_____ Other:

Student Reflection on Work Completed in Advancement Center

What did you accomplish?

Teacher Evaluation of Work Completed in Advancement Center

_____ Student applied goals and completed assignment.
_____ Student understood assignment but needs further assistance to complete.
_____ Student needs further assistance to understand assignment.
_____ Student did not use his or her time productively.
_____ Other comments:

Teacher signature _____

Date _____

Time _____

Advancement Center Weekly Progress Sheet

**(To be completed before each weekly conference
with caseload students)**

Name _____ Date _____

Student Comments

My English class is currently working on:

I specifically need help with:

Plan of action for meeting my goals this week:

Classroom Teacher Comments

Skills that need to be improved:

Assignments Due:

• Assignments are missing, current, or upcoming (circle one).

• I will attend the Advancement Center on (date) _____
  at (time) _____ A.M./P.M.

• Teacher's Signature _____ Date _____

Student Progress Information

**(To be completed each term by classroom teachers
for caseload students)**

Date _____

Student _____

Progress Report Information:

Grade to date:

Comments:

Is visiting the Advancement Center helping this student? Why or why not?

Additional comments:

Student Evaluation of Advancement Center

Name _____ Date _____

1. How often do you visit the Advancement Center? (Circle one.)
   - Never
   - Less than once a month
   - One to three times a month
   - Once a week
   - One to three times a week
   - More than three times a week

2. During which period do you visit the Advancement Center most often?
   1st   2nd   3rd   4th

3. Does the Advancement Center meet your needs?
1	2	3	4	5
No	Somewhat	Adequately	Exceeds	Greatly exceeds

4. Does the Advancement Center provide information and assistance that help you succeed in your regular classroom?
1	2	3	4	5
No	Somewhat	Adequately	Well	Very Well

5. Is the Advancement Center conducive to effective learning?
1	2	3	4	5
No	Somewhat	Adequate	Good	Excellent

6. Is the assistance from the Advancement Center teachers helpful to you?
1	2	3	4	5
No	Somewhat	Adequate	Good	Excellent

7. Specifically, how does the Advancement Center help you succeed in school?
   _____
   _____
   _____

8. Have you participated in any of the Learning Center Enrichment Activities available in the Advancement Center?
   Yes   No
   If yes, which activities?
   _____
   _____

   What are your impressions of the Enrichment Activities? (Do they meet your learning needs? What suggestions do you have for improving the activities? Suggestions for additional activities or centers?)
   _____
   _____
   _____

9. What suggestions do you have for improving the Advancement Center?
   _____
   _____
   _____

Appendix H: Sample Learning Centers

Meaningful Pictures

1. The poetry at this center is written about a common topic. In each poem, the poet describes pictures, snapshots, or photographs. Read the poems at this center, choose one that you like, and draw a sketch of what the poem means to you.

2. Share your sketch with your center partner.

3. Make a list of several pictures that you will bring to school tomorrow to use for writing poetry.

4. Talk about one of your pictures with your center partner.

5. Write a poem.*

6. Share your poem with your center partner.

7. Repeat steps 4, 5, and 6 for each of your pictures.

8. After a few days, revisit your poems and revise as appropriate.

9. Create a way of "displaying" your poems and pictures.

*Variation: In writing about your pictures, you might want to try the format that Kathleen Salapow VanDemark uses in "Snapshots," where she briefly describes several photos, then describes in a series of stanzas (each labeled "snapshot") what can't be seen in the pictures, the struggles and difficulties of growing up—or the approach that Charles Wright uses in "Photographs," where he begins each stanza with the words "One [photograph] of [my father, my mother, me]" and describes each picture in turn before moving in the final stanza to question the unseen portions of the pictures and the lack of explanation of who the people really are.

Postcard Poems

Paul B. Janeczko, editor of *Postcard Poems* (1979), says in his introduction that the poems in this book "are gifts from poets, meant to be shared." He goes on to say that he hopes the poems in his book touch the reader in some way, and he encourages readers to not "let them rest after they've made their impression." Rather, he invites the reader to "let them touch someone else. When you find one that delights you, jot it down on a postcard, or on a note card, or even at the end of a letter."

1. Find a poem in this book, or in another collection at this center, that you would like to send to someone.

2. Jot the poem down on a postcard,* address it, and put it in the mail.

*Variation: As Janeczko suggests, you don't have to limit this sharing to a postcard. You may want to use the poem you find to create a letter, a note card, an e-mail attachment, a poster, or a gift of some type.

Creating an Anthology

Paul Janeczko said, "If you've ever read a book of poetry and noticed poems that touched you more than others, you've taken the first step toward creating a poetry anthology. I look for poems that strike me. These are the ones I save, copying and filling in subject/topic folders. After the poems have sat in the folders for a time, I read through them again to refresh my memory of the poems I've saved. It also helps me make connections, to see similarities and differences in the poems that may help me place them with other poems" (qtd. in Donelson and Nilsen 1997, 345).

1. Each time you visit this center, choose one poem that you really like. (You may also discover poems at other centers, in the library, in a magazines, etc. Start collecting these too.)

2. For each of these poems, write about the thoughts you had while reading it, as well as the thoughts you had after reading it.

3. Save the poems you've chosen and what you've written about them in a folder.

4. Every month or so throughout the term, revisit your folder to refresh your memory of the poems you've saved and to see the connections, similarities, and differences between the poems you've chosen.

5. Several weeks before the end of the term, look through other anthologies as a way to determine how to put your collection together.

6. Gather photographs and artwork, or create drawings, to provide a visual interpretation of each poem.

7. Assemble your anthology, present it to the rest of the class, and leave it at this center until the end of the school year for other students to enjoy.

8. As you visit other student anthologies, write a note to the author about the poems you enjoyed and describe what you learned from the anthology.

Poems for Voices

Paul Fleischman (1988) writes poetry to be read aloud by two people. The lines are divided so that each person has some lines to say alone and others to be said in unison.

1. With a partner, read several of the poems in the book *Joyful Noise: Poems for Two Voices*.

2. Choose a poem that you like from your file of favorites or from the collections at this center and decide how to read it in two or more voices.

3. Rehearse the poem with your partner(s).

4. Share your poem for voices with the class.

5. Leave a copy of your poem at the center for other students to read with a partner.

Poetry from Pictures

As a junior high student, Samantha Abeel (1994) wrote the poems in *Reach for the Moon* from ideas, insights, and images she generated while looking at art.

1. Read several of Samantha's poems and write about one of your favorites.

2. From the picture box or from one of the art books at this center, choose a picture that prompts you to generate ideas, insights, and images.

3. Write a poem based on these thoughts.

4. Display your poem and picture in some way at this center or in the classroom.

Author Study

1. Read several poems written by the same author.

2. Jot down some of the things you notice about the poet's writing that seem to be similar in all of the poems you read. You may want to look at:

   - themes
   - language choices

- rhythm
- rhyme schemes
- length
- layout
- topics
- images
- figurative language

3. Gather information about the poet that may help you to understand how his or her experiences might have influenced the meanings made possible in the poetry.

4. Write a poem in which you try to use the poet's style and one of the themes common to his or her writing.

5. Present the information and ideas you have developed from your investigation to the class and/or create a poetry center.

Poetry Search

1. Find poems from the collections at this center that relate to a theme that the class is studying or one that interests you.

2. Copy several of the poems you like, remembering to give the poet credit.

3. Write several of your own poems using the theme you have been looking for in the poems you have chosen.

4. Gather photographs and artwork, or create drawings, to provide a visual interpretation of each poem.

5. Assemble an anthology,* present it to the rest of the class, and leave it at this center for other students to enjoy.

6. As you visit other anthologies, write a note to the organizer/author about the poems you enjoyed and describe what you learned from the anthology.

*Variations might include the following:

- Create a poster.
- Create a jackdaw (Rasinski and Lehr 1996)—that is, "a collection of anything, real or imaginary, that concretely relates to the book, time, or theme." Elements might range from objects to drawings of imaginary items [or other types of representations]: "food, recipes, clothes or sketches, music or [other] recordings, household gadgets, photographs, poems, maps, . . . biographical sketches of the author and the historical characters, . . . real or facsimile newspaper articles [related to the text's subject

matter], shoe box dioramas of important scenes, or time lines" (64).

War Poetry

Wilfred Owen and Siegfried Sassoon wrote the two poems that influenced Kelly in the book *December Stillness* (Hahn 1988).

1. Read more poetry by these two authors in *The War Poets* (Williams 1976), *The English Poets of the First World War* (Lehmann 1981), and *The Oxford Book of War Poetry* (Stallworthy 1984).

2. Write or talk about some of the common themes or statements each poet is making about war.

3. Choose a poem by one of these authors that stands out for you.

4. Review the art books and photography selections at this center and choose one that seems to go with this poem.

5. Photocopy the poem and photograph on the same page so that it looks like you have prepared a manuscript for publication.

6. On the back or on a separate sheet, write about your reasons for selecting the photograph and poem you chose.

Music Overtly Reflecting Values

1. Read the lyrics from the songs "Blowin' in the Wind" (Bob Dylan), "Fortunate Son" (Creedence Clearwater Revival), "For What It's Worth" (Buffalo Springfield), and "Gun Shy" (10,000 Maniacs).

2. Choose one of the songs and, in your notebook, write about the interests, values, beliefs, or observations revealed in the lyrics. What do you think the song means? What do you think the artist is trying to say in the song? Are the lyrics successful in conveying the underlying message you see in the song?

Works Cited

Abeel, Samantha. 1994. *Reach for the Moon*. Edited by Roberta Williams. Duluth, Minn.: Pfeifer-Hamilton.

Angelou, Maya. 1983. *I Know Why the Caged Bird Sings*. New York: Bantam.

Aronson, Elliot, C. Stephan, J. Sikes, N. Blaney, and M. Snapp. 1978. *The Jigsaw Classroom*. Beverly Hills, Calif.: Sage.

Atwell, Nancie. 1987. *In the Middle: Writing, Reading, and Learning with Adolescents*. Upper Montclair, N.J.: Boynton/Cook.

Brookfield, Stephen D. 1995. *Becoming a Critically Reflective Teacher*. San Francisco: Jossey-Bass.

Buffalo Springfield. 1967. "For What It's Worth." *Buffalo Springfield*. Atlantic.

Burke, Carolyn. September, 1989. "Experience Centers." Handout at "Social Contexts That Support Reading and Writing" workshop. Indiana University Fall Language Arts Conference.

Canady, Robert Lynn, and Michael D. Rettig. 1995. *Block Scheduling: A Catalyst for Change in High Schools*. Princeton, N.J.: Eye on Education.

Canady, Robert Lynn, and Michael D. Rettig. 1996. "All Around the Block: The Benefits and Challenges of a Non-Traditional School Schedule." *The School Administrator* 53.8: 8–14.

Carroll, Joseph. 1990. "The Copernican Plan Evaluated: The Evolution of a Revolution." *Phi Delta Kappan* 76.2: 104–10, 112–13.

Cisneros, Sandra. 1984. *The House on Mango Street*. Houston: Arte Publico Press.

Clavell, James. 1981. *The Children's Story*. New York: Delacorte Press.

Cleland, Janell, and Jodi Wirt. Fall 1995. "Expanding the Role of the Personal Narrative." *Language Arts Journal of Michigan*: 36–46.

Crafton, Linda K. 1982. "Comprehension: Before, During and After Reading." *The Reading Teacher* 36.3: 293–97.

Creedence Clearwater Revival. 1969. "Fortunate Son." *Willy and the Poor Boys*. Fantasy.

Cunningham, R. D., Jr., and S. A. Nogle. 1996. "Implementing a Semesterized Block Schedule: Six Key Elements. *The High School Magazine* 3: 28–30.

Daniels, Harvey. 1994. *Literature Circles: Voice and Choice in the Child-Centered Classroom*. Markham, Ont.: Pembroke.

Dickens, Charles. 1998. *Great Expectations*. New York: Penguin.

Dillard, Annie. 1998. *An American Childhood*. San Francisco: HarperCollins.

Donelson, Kenneth L., and Alleen Pace Nilsen. 1997. *Literature for Today's Young Adults*. 5th ed. New York: Longman.

Dylan, Bob. 1963. "Blowin' in the Wind." *The Freewheelin' Bob Dylan*. Columbia.

Elbow, Peter, and Pat Belanoff. 1989. *A Community of Writers: A Workshop Course in Writing*. New York: McGraw-Hill.

Ferguson, Donald L., Jim Patten, and Bradley Wilson. *Journalism Today*. 5th ed. Lincolnwood, Ill.: National Textbook, 1998.

Fitzgerald, Ron. 1996. "Brain-Compatible Teaching in a Block Schedule."*The School Administrator* 53.8: 20–21, 24.

Fleischman, Paul. 1988. *Joyful Noise: Poems for Two Voices*. New York: HarperTrophy.

Gee, William D. 1997. "The Copernican Plan and Year-Round Education: Two Ideas That Work Together." *Phi Delta Kappan* 78.10: 793–96.

Geismar, Thomas J., and Barbara G. Pullease. 1996. "The Trimester: A Competency Based Model of Block Scheduling: Research Brief." *NASSP Bulletin* 80.581: 95–105.

Hackmann, Donald G. 1995. "Ten Guidelines for Implementing Block Scheduling." *Educational Leadership* 53.3: 24–27.

Hahn, Mary Downing. 1988. *December Stillness*. New York: Clarion.

Hanson, Linda. 1992. Personal Conversation.

Harste, Jerome C., and Kathy G. Short, with Carolyn Burke. 1988. *Creating Classrooms for Authors: The Reading-Writing Connection*. Portsmouth, N.H.: Heinemann.

Ibsen, Henrik. 1992. *A Doll's House*. New York: Dover.

Illinois State Board of Education Superintendent's Bulletin. 22 January 1997. No. 97S-09.

Janeczko, Paul B., ed. 1979. *Postcard Poems: A Collection of Poetry for Sharing*. New York: Bradbury.

Kerr, M. E. 1983. "Where Are You Now, William Shakespeare?" *ME, ME, ME, ME, ME: Not a Novel*. New York: Harper & Row.

Knowles, John. 1975. *A Separate Peace*. New York: Bantam.

Lehmann, John. 1981. *The English Poets of the First World War*. New York: Thames and Hudson.

Macrorie, Ken. 1988. *The I-Search Paper*. Portsmouth, N.H.: Boynton/Cook.

Manzo, Anthony. 1969. "The ReQuest Procedure." *Journal of Reading* 13.2: 123–26.

Mathabane, Mark. 1998. *Kaffir Boy: The True Story of a Black Youth's Coming of Age in Apartheid South Africa*. New York: Simon & Schuster.

Ogle, Donna M. 1986. "K-W-L: A Teaching Model That Develops Active Reading of Expository Text." *The Reading Teacher* 39: 564–70.

Owens, Jesse. 1970. "Open Letter to a Young Negro." In *Blackthink: My Life as Black Man and White Man* by Jesse Owens with Paul G. Neimark. New York: Morrow.

Porter, Carol, and Janell Cleland. 1995. *The Portfolio as a Learning Strategy.* Portsmouth, N.H.: Boynton/Cook.

Rasinski, Timothy V., and Susan Lehr. 1996. "The Jackdaw Way." Pp. 64–65 in *Teaching Reading and Literature, Grades 4–6.* Standards Consensus Series. Urbana, Ill.: NCTE.

Romano, Tom. 1987. *Clearing the Way: Working with Teenage Writers.* Portsmouth, N.H.: Heinemann.

Schoenstein, Roger. 1995. "The New School on the Block." *The Executive Educator* 17.8: 18–21.

Short, Kathy G., and Carolyn Burke. *Creating Curriculum: Teachers and Students as a Community of Learners.* Portsmouth, N.H.: Heinemann, 1991.

Shortt, Thomas, and Yvonne V. Thayer. 1997. "A Vision for Block Scheduling: Where Are We Now? Where Are We Going?" *NASSP Bulletin* 81.593: 1–15.

Silverstein, Shel. 1964. *The Giving Tree.* New York: Harper & Row.

Smith, Karen. 1995. "Bringing Children and Literature Together in the Elementary Classroom." *Primary Voices K–6* 3.2: 22–32.

Stallworthy, Jon, ed. 1984. *The Oxford Book of War Poetry.* Oxford: Oxford University Press.

Tafel, Linda. June 1992. Personal Conversation.

10,000 Maniacs. 1987. "Gun Shy." *In My Tribe.* Elektra.

Tierney, Robert J., John E. Readence, and Ernest K. Dishner. 1995. *Reading Strategies and Practices: A Compendium.* 4th ed. Boston: Allyn and Bacon.

Volavková, Hana, ed. 1993. *I Never Saw Another Butterfly: Children's Drawings and Poems from Terezín Concentration Camp 1942–1944.* 2d ed. New York: Schocken.

Vygotsky, L. S. 1978. *Mind in Society: The Development of Higher Psychological Processes.* Cambridge, Mass.: Harvard University Press.

Watson, Dorothy. 1978. "Reader Selected Miscues: Getting More from Sustained Silent Reading." *English Education* 10.1: 75–85.

Watson, Dorothy, Carolyn Burke, and Jerome Harste. 1989. *Whole Language: Inquiring Voices.* Richmond Hill, Ont.: Scholastic.

Wiesel, Elie. 1960. *Night.* New York: Bantam.

Wiggins, Grant. 1989. "Teaching to the (Authentic) Test." *Educational Leadership* 46.7: 41–47.

Williams, Oscar, ed. 1976. *The War Poets: An Anthology of the War Poetry of the 20th Century.* Miami, Fla.: Granger.

Wyatt, Linda D. 1996. "More Time, More Training." *The School Administrator* 53.8: 16–18.

Author

Carol Porter taught reading and English classes at Mundelein High School before accepting a position as assistant professor in the secondary education program at National-Louis University, where she teaches general methods and English language arts courses to preservice middle school and high school teachers. Currently Porter is also teaching reading at Deerfield High School. Her publications include *The Portfolio as a Learning Strategy,* coauthored with Janell Cleland, and chapters in *Talking about Books: Creating Literate Communities* and (with Linda K. Crafton) *Delicate Balances: Collaborative Research in Language Education.* In addition to working with schools and teachers who are preparing to implement alternative schedules, Porter conducts reading workshops for middle school and high school teachers wanting to improve the literacy skills of their adolescent readers. Her doctoral work informed, and her current high school teaching position continues to inform, her understanding of the reading process and of strategies that can be used with secondary students. For the past three years, she has been a member of NCTE's Reading Commission.

Contributors

Karen M. Hall taught Theatre 1, Theatre 2, Technical Theatre, Choir, and Music Theory during her four-year tenure at Mundelein High School. She also directed and designed three productions per year. Her production of *All in the Timing* was selected as a full-length production to be performed at the 1999 Illinois High School Theatre Festival. Hall received a B.F.A. in musical theatre from Syracuse University and an M.A. in performing arts from Emerson College. She is currently completing her Ed.D. in curriculum and instruction at Loyola University. She has authored numerous articles on acting and musical theatre and frequently presents at conferences and festivals. Since 2000, Hall has been teaching Speech and Drama at Maine Township High School East in Park Ridge, Illinois.

Diane VonderHaar teaches English and journalism at Mundelein High School, Mundelein, Illinois, and is responsible for the production of both the school newspaper and the yearbook. She holds a master's degree in curriculum and instruction. She also teaches Advanced Placement English and speaks at conferences on teaching literary theory to high school students.

This book was typeset in Palatino and Helvetica by Electronic Imaging.
The typefaces used on the cover were Albertus, Officina Sans,
Officina Serif, and Trebuchet.
The book was printed on 50-lb. Husky Offset by IPC Communication Services.